Together in God's Service

TOWARD A THEOLOGY OF ECCLESIAL LAY MINISTRY

PAPERS FROM A COLLOQUIUM

National Conference of Catholic Bishops
Subcommittee on Lay Ministry
Committee on the Laity

Together in God's Service: Toward a Theology of Ecclesial Lay Ministry, Papers from a Colloquium was a project of the bishops' Subcommittee on Lay Ministry of the Committee on the Laity. It was approved for publication by the members of the Subcommittee and by the members of the Committee on the Laity. It is authorized for publication by the undersigned.

Monsignor Dennis M. Schnurr
General Secretary
NCCB/USCC

First printing, August 1998

ISBN 1-57455-285-6

Contents

Foreword

This book contains materials from the Theological Colloquium: "Toward a Theology of Ecclesial Lay Ministry," which was held at the University of Dayton, May 11–12, 1997. The colloquium was part of the Leadership for Ecclesial Lay Ministry Project of the National Conference of Catholic Bishops Subcommittee on Lay Ministry.

The first purpose of the project, funded by a grant from the Lilly Endowment, was to provide information and other forms of assistance to diocesan bishops and their advisors/collaborators in order for them to understand the implications and scope of the phenomenon of ecclesial lay ministry in the United States and to enhance their abilities for leadership in related areas. The early initiatives of the project (surveys, focus groups, forum with professional ministerial associations) identified the necessity of a more adequate theological basis for ecclesial lay ministry. The colloquium was a major effort to address that area, which the bishops identified as a priority.

Participants at the colloquium were identified and invited by the subcommittee on the basis of their theological competence and particular interest. The subcommittee also was intentional about bringing together a group that represented a mixture of backgrounds (lay, religious, clerical), ethnic origins, and theological viewpoints. A list of the participants is included with these materials.

The goals of the colloquium were (1) to advance an articulation of the theological issues raised by the experience of ecclesial lay ministry; (2) to recommend next steps for the subcommittee to foster the development of ecclesial lay ministry; and (3) to model how bishops and academic and pastoral theologians can work together in fostering the mission of Jesus Christ.

1

In preparation for the colloquium, the nine papers that make up the bulk of these materials were written and distributed to the participants. The participants read the papers before coming to Dayton and sent questions (also included with these materials) for discussion that were grouped by the staff into six categories. The process for the colloquium included small-group discussions based on the six categories in addition to general discussions.

These papers have already been distributed to all the bishops of the National Conference of Catholic Bishops. We publish them now for a wider audience in the hope that they will be a resource for all those reflecting on the issues they address.

We are grateful to the steering committee for the colloquium: Zeni Fox, Ph.D., chair; James L. Heft, SM, Ph.D.; Bishop Gerald Kicanas; David Power, OMI, S.T.D.; Elissa Rinere, CP, J.C.D.; and Bishop Emil Wcela. We are also grateful to the writers of these papers and to each of the participants whose contributions made for a stimulating and fruitful colloquium. Finally, we are grateful to the Lilly Endowment, whose support has made this project possible.

NCCB Subcommittee on Lay Ministry
Most Reverend Phillip F. Straling, Chairman
Most Reverend Tod D. Brown
Most Reverend John C. Dunne
Most Reverend James R. Hoffman
Most Reverend Gerald Kicanas
Most Reverend Edward U. Kmiec
Most Reverend Armando Ochoa
Most Reverend Emil Wcela

Ecclesial Lay Ministers:
An Overview   BY ZENI FOX, PH.D.

The U.S. bishops have chosen the term "ecclesial minister" to describe lay people who have professionally prepared for ministry; no fuller definition exists. Therefore, in order to describe these new ministers in a preliminary way, this paper draws upon sociological studies that use various parameters.

What they do in ministry, demographic data, paths to ministry education and formation, support for them and their ministry, supervision, collegiality, and theological self-understanding are presented. Throughout, ecclesiastical and theological questions that emerge from the data are posed.

(This paper is a summary of chapters 1-4 in a larger published work by the author: *New Ecclesial Ministers* [Kansas City, Mo.: Sheed and Ward, 1997].)

Preface

The purpose of this paper is to describe, as phenomenologically as possible, "ecclesial lay ministers." The first draft was critiqued by the steering committee, the second by representatives of lay associations and organizations. The purpose of the consultations was to ask whether this overview reflects our experience of ecclesial lay ministry in the Church in the United States, and can serve as a valid starting point for the work of the colloquium. Overwhelmingly, the response was that, in general, the paper does reflect the present situation. Furthermore, it has been strengthened by the suggestions from the consultations.

Introduction

In 1980, the U.S. Catholic bishops wrote *Called and Gifted*. In it, they described the laity's call to ministry and in that context commented on a new phenomenon that they observed in their dioceses: "lay persons who have prepared for professional ministry in the Church." They called these laity "ecclesial ministers."[1] However, no description of their preparation or roles was given. Still today, the boundaries for defining who is and who is not an ecclesial minister have not been drawn. As we strive to reflect theologically on this new reality at the colloquium, the issues involved in definition—in delineation—will confront us, although that is not our primary task. In writing this paper, therefore, it is necessary to make some arbitrary decisions and to describe ecclesial lay ministers in what can only be a limited way. Our corporate reflection on what is happening will enable us to engage more adequately in this task of describing and defining.

Most of the sociological research that has been done studies ecclesial lay ministers working in ministerial roles in parishes; therefore, most of what is presented in this paper is about parish ministers. The existing research uses varying norms for defining the populations to be studied. One norm is usually employment, but often both part-time and full-time ministers are considered. However, some formal leaders volunteer their services, even "full time." Some studies include ministers who are members of religious communities; others do not. Sometimes persons in a particular ministry position are considered; sometimes the focus is on those exercising leadership in the parish community; and sometimes a credential delineates who is part of the sample. In an effort simply to look at what is happening in the Church, I will present this research without an evaluation of the norms, but I will indicate what they are in the endnotes. (Of course there is a danger in this "blending" of diverse studies.) At the colloquium, we can assess the theological implications of what we see and can strive to define the category we are considering.

What They Do: Positions in Ministry

One way to approach a description of ecclesial lay ministers is by studying some new roles that have emerged in the Church in the United States since the Second Vatican Council. The oldest is that of the director of religious education (although nomenclature varies); the first DREs date to the mid-1960s. (It is worth noting that these developments pre-date a perceived clergy shortage, as well as the decline in numbers of vowed religious.) Studies of DREs often emphasize that they are professionals with master's degrees in a relevant field.[2]

By the mid-1980s, a study of persons professionally employed in parishes found that in addition to DREs, there were youth ministers, pastoral ministers, directors of liturgy, and directors of social concerns, as well as several positions unique to particular parishes.[3] The 1992 study *New Parish Ministers*, which was conducted for the NCCB, states that various roles in the ministry of religious education are the most prevalent, and pastoral associates or pastoral ministers the second most widely found. Liturgists, youth ministers, music ministers, and other less frequently identified roles (e.g., ministry to the elderly, evangelization) are also described.[4] Pastoral administrators or parish directors (again, nomenclature varies), who are responsible for the pastoral care of parishes, fill another role,[5] perhaps in less than 1 percent of our parishes,[6] though other studies suggest a larger number.[7] Persons whose primary responsibility is service to the needy are found very infrequently in parishes.

In dioceses, lay people serve in roles such as chancellor, superintendent of schools, and chief administrative officer; and as directors and staff of offices such as religious education, worship, and lay formation. The National Association of Church Personnel Administrators believes that "The average worker in the coming decade will be lay, and many will be from minority groups." Ongoing training will be essential, because "It can no longer be assumed that the seminary and the sister formation program have prepared workers."[8]

Neither statistical nor descriptive studies of lay persons serving in Catholic institutional ministries (e.g., presidents, campus ministers, and chaplains) are available.[9] However, we know that these roles are increasingly filled by lay people. For example, of the Catholic Campus Ministry Association's 1,800 members, one-half are not ordained,[10] and of the 3,547 members of the National Association of Catholic Chaplains, 5 percent are lay men, 21 percent lay women, and 50 percent vowed religious.[11] (It is worth noting that priests and vowed religious work within structured patterns of relationship to the official Church; priests are assigned directly and vowed religious traditionally undertake ministries within a diocese at the invitation of the bishop. There is no formal relationship between lay leaders in institutional ministries and the local Church.)

5

The picture that emerges is of many laity and vowed religious serving in various formal leadership roles that once would have been reserved for clergy. Furthermore, the roles represent a diversity of ministries. These roles are found within the Church's pastoral, educational, and liturgical ministries and encompass functions such as setting direction, oversight, ministerial formation, and pastoral care.

What They Do: Functions and Responsibilities

It is interesting to observe the variety of responsibilities that individuals filling particular positions may actually have. Among DREs, for example, most are responsible for catechist training, but some also minister to the aging (11%) or to the divorced and grieving (15%). More than 90 percent work with elementary school children, but less than 20 percent with young adults.[12] Philip Murnion notes that among pastoral associates, there is no particular ministry for which more than one-half in the sample are leaders. Their activities may include evangelization, home visiting, and ministry training, for example.[13] In fact, one study found that the correlation between job titles and ministry activities was so weak that it was more helpful to group ministers according to the ministry activities they perform. Using cluster analysis, the categories that emerged were the following: Ministry Administrators, Liturgists and Musicians, Religious Educators, and Helping and Service Ministers.[14] Individual pastors and parishes, and individual ministers, shape the defining of the tasks performed. What does become clear is that the definition of positions is local and particular.

Another study asked lay ministers to choose from a list of eighteen the three functions most important for their work and for priests' work. The overwhelming majority indicated that eucharistic celebrant is primary for priests, with community builder ranked a distant second. No other function received a significant preference. For themselves, the lay ministers ranked as primary community builder and gave significant importance to enabler of leaders, administrator, and teacher.[15] Perhaps this is faintly representative of ways lay ministers are trying to differentiate their functions and responsibilities from those of priests.

Who They Are, Demographically

Overwhelmingly, the new parish ministers are women. Murnion's study indicates they are 85 percent of the new ministers, and approximately the same percentage has been found in other studies.[16] However, a study in which two-thirds of the respondents worked in dioceses found that one-third were men,[17] and the proportion of men is higher in youth ministry (41%) and music ministry (52%).[18]

It may be that salary influences this gender pattern. Asked "if you were to leave church work, what would be the reasons," men ranked inadequate salary first, whereas women ranked it third. Furthermore, almost half the respondents said their salary "provides supplementary income for my family," and only 8 percent said that they were the primary support of their family. Men also ranked as important "lack of security" (third) and "lack of advancement possibilities" (fifth), items women did not consider significant.[19] In our culture, men have traditionally been socialized to value personal achievement, so lack of advancement possibilities as well as inadequate salary may be deterrents for men in the United States.

When vowed religious are excluded, almost two thirds of parish lay ministers are married; 6 percent are widowed, divorced, or separated. Furthermore, 71 percent have children, with family size slightly higher than in the general population. Sometimes, both husband and wife are employed by the Church, occasionally in one setting. The presence of significant numbers of married people among the Church's ministers represents a change with implications for the life of the Church, both pastorally (these ministers, by reason of their social location, bring a lay perspective to their work)[20] and organizationally (existing models of ministry often presume celibate life and do not respect the demands of family life).[21]

Among the new parish ministers, 42 percent are members of religious congregations—mostly women religious.[22] And, although the numbers of vowed religious are declining, trends suggest that many will continue to seek opportunities to serve in pastoral roles.[23] Of course, many issues associated with ministry are quite different for lay and vowed religious persons, including such varied ones as ministerial identity and retirement concerns.

The great majority of the new ministers who are not vowed religious are in their mid-thirties to mid-fifties, with a median age of 45. Women religious in ministry are considerably older, with 40 percent over age sixty, 25 percent over sixty-five and a median age of fifty-eight.[24] However, youth ministers tend to be younger; two thirds are under thirty-five, although there are also a significant number who are over fifty. (Many of the latter have only begun their jobs in the last five years; the stereotype of youth ministers necessarily being young people does not hold).[25] Furthermore, the profile of graduate students in ministry suggests that this general age pattern will continue.[26] Why many people in their twenties are not becoming involved in ministry bears study. Comparison of age data for laity with that for priests (median age 55)[27] also bears reflection.

The overwhelming majority of new ministers are white; every study confirms this. *New Parish Ministers* found 95 percent white, almost 4 percent Hispanic, less than 1 percent African American, and .5 percent Asian or Native American.[28] Graduate ministry program participants are 87.7 percent white, 3.7 percent Asian-Pacific, 3 percent African American, 3.2 percent Hispanic and 1 percent Native American.[29] Diocesan programs draw a stronger percentage of Hispanics, 15 percent.[30] Of course, the professional model, which our term *ecclesial minister* gives us, may not be the most helpful for describing developments in lay leadership in African American, Asian, and Hispanic communities,[31] and perhaps even in rural communities.[32]

Paths to Ministry

What brings lay people to employment as parish ministers? One important finding is that as many as 90 percent of employed ministers had originally been parish volunteers. For lay people, the transition to employment often comes at the invitation of the pastor. With women religious, many are hired through their congregations' clearinghouse services or contacts, or diocesan clearinghouse efforts. While the pastor is the most important person in the hiring process, councils and their committees also play a role and contribute to defining both the position and the qualifications.[33]

Why do people accept employment in ministry? Among DREs, the responses most often given to this question—posed in an open-ended fashion—can be described as a desire to share the faith. Wanting to preach the Gospel, to spread the Kingdom, and to serve the Church by sharing the Good News of salvation are some examples. The second most important reason was that they were asked by the pastor.[34]

When asked who was most influential in their choice of church work, a strong majority responded that it was an individual priest. Second most influential was the individual's spouse. (Since one-third of the sample was unmarried, this has greater importance than the statistic alone suggests.) Lay ministers also ranked high as influential in their choice—an interesting factor in light of the relatively small number of lay ministers.[35]

Asked to identify factors that influenced their choice of ministry, youth ministers overwhelmingly indicated it was concern about youth and their needs (87%). Their own lack of opportunities as a youth for involvement in the Church was named by 27 percent. Although they could check any that applied, other choices had less than a one-fourth response: high school retreat (22%), experience as a parent (16%), college campus ministry program (14%), college theology classes (12%), Catholic high school experience (11%), parish high school religion classes (9%), and college retreat (7%).[36]

When people make choices about work in life, they often do so because someone models the role. Among lay ministers, slightly more than one-half said they had a model for their role in the Church. Of these, more than one-half said this was a lay person employed in a parish, and one-third said that the person worked in a diocesan office. Vowed religious influenced one third.[37] Laity are influencing lay people to choose ecclesial ministry.

The reasons people continue in ministry also help to explain their choice. Asked to rank thirteen possible reasons for staying in church work, lay ministers clearly chose three as most important: they enjoy the work, feel called to it, and think it utilizes gifts God has given them. Somewhat less significant was that they contribute to a need that must be addressed. Ranked lowest of the thirteen reasons were "I need the salary" and "my position has security."[38]

The profile that emerges is of lay persons externally influenced by both parish priests and other lay ministers and internally motivated by a sense of vocation to the work and a desire to serve and to use God-given gifts.

Education and Formation of Ecclesial Ministers

Generally speaking, the new ministers are well educated—certainly more so than the population in general. Eighty percent have at least a college education; more than one-half hold a master's degree, and 1.5 percent a doctorate. However, among the laity only 30 percent hold a master's degree, whereas among the religious, 77 percent do. Almost all those who do not have a college degree are lay.[39] The great majority of lay ministers (87%) have taken part in nondegree programs related to their ministry, one-half of which were sponsored by dioceses. Sixty percent have some type of certification.[40]

However, in contrast to the preparation of priests, there is no standard program of studies. For example, among youth ministers, only 9 percent at the undergraduate level and 7 percent at the graduate level completed degrees in theology or religious studies. Youth Ministry Certificate programs do not always include a theological component. Furthermore, only about one-half of the youth ministers attended Catholic high school, and less than one-half a Catholic college, so their exposure to Catholic culture is limited. And youth ministers do not think theological education that important for effective work with youth, valuing youth ministry education as more important.[41]

Whereas traditionally dioceses and religious orders have borne the cost of ministry education, the cost for the education of lay ministers falls to individual ministers and parishes. Almost one-half indicated that they, or their families, funded their education. The parish underwrote the cost for 28 percent, and part of the cost for 17 percent. Parishes are most likely to fund certificate study.[42]

Formation for ministry, with its emphasis on personal and spiritual development, is a valued aspect of preparation for priesthood and religious life. Programs for laity also include formation opportunities; most offer a combination of academic study, ministerial skills development, spiritual formation, and supervised field experience. Formation opportunities include eucharistic liturgies, prayer/reflection groups, prayer services, retreats, days of recollection, and spiritual advisors. However, "twice as much time is given to spiritual formation of participants in nondegree programs as in degree programs."[43] In fact, directors of graduate programs sometimes disagree with the idea of making spiritual formation a component, and the majority do not require participation. As one director said, "our students have their faith communities in which we encourage them to participate."[44]

Support for the New Ministers
The Notre Dame Study of Catholic Parish Life indicates that active Catholics believe that fostering religious education of children and teenagers, helping poor people in the parish, making converts and/or reclaiming church dropouts, and enhancing the religious education of adults are their highest priorities.[45] Other than Sunday Mass, the programs parishes are most likely to offer are grade school and high school religious education.[46] And the personal needs or family problems they would most turn to the parish for assistance with are the religious education of children and of themselves.[47] The new ministers often have responsibility for these areas of church life, performing functions, therefore, that the community values. Studies probing Catholics' judgments as to whether lay people rightfully should be performing such functions show that a high level of acceptance exists among lay people in general, pastors and other priests, and Catholic college students.[48]

The new ministers themselves report both that the pastor, pastoral team, or parish council had delegated authority to them for their ministry (77% said "yes, a great deal") and that their authority is accepted (by 95% of staff and 97% of parishioners). These ministers affirm that they are functioning as leaders in their parish situations: 70 percent to a great extent, 27 percent somewhat.[49] Even those who provide pastoral care for parishes without a resident priest are accepted by their communities.[50]

Parish leaders and members say that the new ministers are contributing positively to parish life. Given a list of twenty-five aspects of parish ministry, in every category 50 to 90 percent of respondents (pastors, parishioners, and other staff) said that they had "added considerably" or made "some improvement." Pastors valued contributions devolving both from particular competencies (e.g., "improvement of religious education") and ministerial skills (e.g., "enable parishioners to feel at home"); parishioners, too, valued competencies (e.g., "improvement of liturgy/worship") but also valued the lay contribution (e.g., "sensitivity to family needs"). The researchers conclude: "the parish ministers have made an enormous contribution to parish life, by their abilities as well as their numbers. In the eyes of all involved they have enhanced parish life in almost all respects."[51]

However, despite all of these positive indicators, when lay ministers were asked to rank ways their work situations could be improved, "that my efforts are valued" ranked first by a significant margin. "That my role or function be clarified" and "that people thought more highly of my role" ranked second and third. Other possible choices—more money, security, success, and autonomy—were all ranked considerably lower.[52] Appreciation of their work and role seems to be a significant need for these new ministers.

Another dimension of support is personal, emotional support needed when difficulties are encountered. At these times, lay ministers turn primarily to spouses, family, and friends, not to the pastor or other staff members.[53] Just as the realization of the importance of deacons' wives has grown gradually in training programs, so, too, the networks of support for lay ministers need to be reflected on more. Additional support comes from professional memberships and informal networking with colleagues. Most meet with others at least once a month,[54] thereby gaining personal and professional support—and also developing an ecclesial identity.

Salary and benefits are another aspect of support. The most recent comprehensive study we have for parish ministers included members of religious orders; the average for full-time persons was $15,000 to $20,000 [55]—considerably less than the educational level of the group would suggest. The National Association of Church Business Administration, an ecumenical group, reports a higher range for Catholics employed in diocesan offices in positions such as Christian Education Minister and Music Minister/Director. Average salaries range from $24,777 to $36,400, depending on the position—considerably lower than the averages for similar positions in Protestant churches.[56] For close to one-half of the ministers, their salary "provides supplementary income for the family." Only 8 percent are the primary support of a family; 24 percent support themselves.[57] One minister observed, "Men are forced to leave ministry if they intend to marry and have a family. Women stay, if it's a second income."[58] Salary issues are important for vowed religious also, especially in light of the increasing number of retired sisters and brothers.

In U.S. society, health care coverage and pension benefits are important. One study found that 9 percent of diocesan and parish employees said they receive no health care/insurance benefits.[59] Pension plans are usually diocesan. A consequence of this is that a minister who moves from one diocese to another (not unusual in our highly mobile society) loses the benefits accrued from membership in the retirement plan.

Despite some difficulties with clarification of their roles, or salary or benefit problems, lay ministers say they are happy in the work they do in the Church—90 percent are happy, 44 percent of whom are *very* happy.[60] Overwhelmingly, they said their ministry is satisfying, gives a sense of accomplishment, and is spiritually rewarding.[61] When asked to rank reasons they would continue in church work, the highest ranked response was that they enjoy the work.[62] Furthermore, 72 percent said they would continue as volunteers in the Church if they left ministry work, and only 3 percent said they would not.[63] Finally, when asked about their intentions regarding continuing in ministry, 38 percent said they planned to stay indefinitely, an equal number were unsure about how long they would stay, and one-sixth planned to leave in three years or less. There were positive correlations between those planning to leave and saying their salary was not fair, and also between those planning to stay indefinitely and saying they are very happy in their work.[64]

The pattern that emerges is of good support from the parish community for the new ministers and the work they do. And yet somehow the support is insufficient, as shown by the ministers' strong desire that their efforts be valued more and their roles be better clarified. Despite this, the new ministers are happy in their work, and many intend to continue indefinitely.

Supervision in Ministry

In many instances, ecclesial ministers are role initiators in their parishes. Often, they are in their first church-related job, and sometimes their first job. However, studies show that supervision (active, ongoing oversight and evaluation of their work) is not generally given. Approximately one-third of lay ministers and less than one-half of youth ministers (the youngest, least experienced of the new ministers) report that they receive supervision. Furthermore, criteria for evaluation are developed in far fewer cases. Generally, it is the pastor who evaluates.[65] Of course, since accountability procedures have usually not been well developed in parishes, this data is not surprising. However, the informal mechanisms of "supervision" provided in rectories and convents by older, more experienced ministers who informally guided new ministers are not available for ecclesial lay ministers.

An interesting fact that emerges from the data is that many lay ministers think that evaluation should be conducted by a committee of parishioners. In fact, when asked whose evaluation they most often seek, the highest ranked choice was those they serve. In addition, those they serve are the most valued source of praise, the locus of the most painful critique, the ones they most often seek evaluation from, and those they estimate as most valuing the work they do. Finally, the needs of the people was ranked first when stating what gives general guidance as they plan their work day by day. A positive valuation of this data is that it clearly shows a diaconal focus in their ministry. However, a caution could be noted: the diocesan office and the bishop were ranked lowest of all categories.[66] This could reflect the lack of relationship between ecclesial ministers and the diocese. As Murnion has said, "for all our protests that ministry in the Catholic community is not congregational, the dynamics in place are leading to an increasingly local or congregational source and shaping of parish ministry."[67] This lack of relationship is due to structural realities, not interpersonal ones.

Collegial Patterns of Ministry

Ecclesial ministers believe in collegiality. Asked if it is a desirable goal for the Church, 90 percent said yes, both for the diocesan and the universal Church. Furthermore, their practice reflects their theology. Only 7 percent said they make work decisions alone. Usually their shared decision-making is with the staff (the pastor and/or other staff), less frequently with the people. Only about 20 percent include parishioners in decision-making processes, though among youth ministers this number doubles.[68]

The new ministers invite parishioners to be involved in many different ministerial roles, and the people usually say yes.[69] Ecclesial ministers work with various groups, including committees, planning teams, and advisory boards. Only 13 percent say they do not work with such a group, and 75 percent personally have formed one.[70] More people are involved ministerially and in collegially shaping the direction of ministry because of the work of these ministers.

Theological Self-Understanding

While it is difficult to make judgments about people's theological self-understanding from statistical data, it is helpful to explore some ways ecclesial ministers respond to questions that have theological significance. In a survey that consistently used the phrase "church work," respondents were asked to choose the word that described their employment in the Church. Sixty percent chose *ministry*, an additional 13 percent chose other words associated with church mission: *vocation, discipleship, apostolate.* Ten percent chose *profession* and 9 percent chose other words associated with secular work (*position, job, role*).[71] As John Coleman, a Jesuit sociologist, has observed, the word "ministry" was being used without an effort to define it, and it served as a motivational symbol.[72] It is worth noting that the use of the term

15

"lay ministry" predates use of the term "presbyteral ministry" in Catholic periodicals in the period since the Second Vatican Council. Laity appear to have chosen the term not because of its association with priesthood but probably because of its New Testament origins.

Almost three-fourths of lay ministers affirm that they have received charisms, defined in the survey as special gifts of grace for service in the Church. A more indirect indication of this same reality is glimpsed in their response to a question asking why they would continue in church work. As noted above, enjoying the work, feeling called to the work, using God-given gifts, and contributing to a need were the strongest responses.

As shown above, the new ministers think that the authority they need to exercise their roles is delegated to them, and accepted by the parishioners. The ministers also state that they function as leaders in their settings. When asked to rank the order of what gives them their authority for their work in the Church, they responded "baptism" and "confirmation" with a strong preference. Professional training and competence were ranked second, and a vocation from God third. Being hired, a mandate from the community, a mandate from parish priest(s), and a commissioning or investiture (in that order) were ranked significantly lower. Interestingly, in response to the same question about priests, their responses were: a vocation from God, holy orders, and baptism and confirmation. Seminary training did not rank significantly high, in contrast to their emphasis on their professional training.[73] There are some apparent theological contradictions here; they emerge from the survey data itself. Of course, the experience of priests appointed because of ordination and laity hired because of competence may also be influencing this pattern.[74]

When asked whether their work in the Church implies a permanent commitment, perhaps analogous to that of a permanent deacon, 40 percent said yes, 40 percent said no. A cross tabulation with the 40 percent of the group who said that they plan to stay in church ministry indefinitely showed that the majority of those who say it is a permanent commitment plan to stay indefinitely.[75] This, therefore, is a group of individuals who view their work in the Church in a sense as a state of life.

Lay ministers were asked whether they would choose a rite of installation in their role, if there were one. Forty percent said yes, and 34 percent perhaps; only 14 percent said no. A cross tabulation indicates that 24 percent of the total sample both plan to stay indefinitely and would choose a rite of installation. On the other hand, only 7 percent said they had a formal commissioning service.[76] Of course, except for installation as lector or acolyte (for men only), no official rite exists.

The statistics indicate that the commitment the ministers envision is generally as lay persons. Only 4 percent say they had not yet made a final decision about seeking ordination or entering religious life. Forty percent had never considered these options; others had seriously considered them (17%) or had begun to prepare and did not continue (13%) or left after ordination or vows (12%).[77]

Ecclesial ministers do not think that the primary reason they are employed is because of a shortage of priests or of women religious. Those reasons were ranked third and fourth. The first two reasons, by a strong margin, were that the community recognizes the need for the areas of specialization for which they are trained and that a variety of gifts are given to various members of the community.[78] Perhaps the first reason is shaped by the increasing specialization found in the larger culture, and the second by a memory of the variety of gifts and ministries found in the New Testament communities.

Conclusion

The purpose of the colloquium is that we engage in theological dialogue and discernment about the phenomenon—ecclesial lay ministry—that has emerged in the life of the Church in the United States. The reality invites us to ask, What questions does this data pose to our understanding of ministry? What does it mean? It also invites us to ask, What questions does ecclesial lay ministry pose to our present church practice? In light of this new reality, what ought we to do?

Notes

1. National Conference of Catholic Bishops, *Called and Gifted: The American Catholic Laity.* (Washington, D.C.: United States Catholic Conference, 1980), p. 5. In the consultation on this paper with lay associations, the omission of lay teachers in parish Catholic schools was mentioned. "It is important that we not separate the ministry of Catholic education from other ecclesial ministries in the parish" (Msgr. John Unger, Catholic Education Office, St. Louis). In light of the fact that the bishops named ecclesial ministers a *new* development in 1980, they apparently did not include Catholic school teachers. Whether they should be included is, of course, not resolved; however, the research used in this paper will not include them.

2. See, for example, Thomas P. Walters, *National Profile of Professional Religious Education Coordinators/Directors* (Washington, D.C.: National Conference of Diocesan Directors, 1983), p. 4. Professional is defined as "A person with a master's degree and at least three years of administration or teaching experience" (p. 4). See also Thomas P. Walters, Wayne Smith, and Sylvia Marotta, *A Hopeful Horizon* (Washington, D.C.: National Catholic Educational Association, 1993), esp. pp. 35–39.

3. Zeni Fox, *A Post-Vatican II Phenomenon: Lay Ministries: A Critical Three-Dimensional Study* (unpublished dissertation, Fordham University, 1986). A summary of the sociological data (one part of the larger study) is found in "The New Parish Ministers," *CHURCH* (Spring 1991: 16–21). The population studied was lay persons employed part time or full time in parishes, using a national sample developed by seeking names through a representative sample of dioceses.

4. Philip J. Murnion (New York: National Pastoral Life Center, 1992), pp. 43–54. The population studied was lay persons and vowed religious employed in parishes, using a national sample developed by seeking names directly from parishes. Murnion reports that 76 percent of parishes have a religious educator, 25 percent a general parish minister, 18 percent a musician/music director, 15 percent a youth minister, and 10 percent a liturgy/liturgy-music director.

5. Peter Gilmour, *The Emerging Pastor: Non-Ordained Catholic Pastors* (Kansas City, Mo.: Sheed and Ward, 1986). Pastoral administrators, deacons, vowed religious, and lay are included in this study.

6. Murnion, p. vi.

7. See, for example, Ruth A. Wallace, "Women Pastoral Administrators: Reflections from Interviews," *CHURCH*, (Fall 1991): 43. She posits that in 1991, 2 percent of parishes were headed by pastoral administrators.

8. Ann Margaret O'Hara, ed., *Attitudinal Survey on Working in the Catholic Church: An Executive Summary* (Cincinnati: National Association of Church Personnel Administrators, 1991), p. 18.

9. A valuable study of this topic is *The Future of Catholic Institutional Ministries*, by Charles J. Fahey and Mary Ann Lewis (New York: Third Age Center, Fordham University, 1992).

10. Statistics provided by Donald McCrabb, executive director, at a Forum of Lay Ministerial Associations, convened by the Subcommittee on Lay Ministry, March 16, 1996.

11. Statistics provided by Robert Kopchinski, director, in a telephone conversation November 11, 1996, based on their September 1996 statistics.

12. Walters, pp. 23–24.

13. Murnion, pp. 48, 53–54.

14. David De Lambo and Sue Weber, *Lay Ministry Study* ([Arch]Dioceses of Indianapolis, Evansville, Gary, and Lafayette in Indiana, 1995).

15. Fox (1986), pp. 243–247.

16. Murnion, p. 27; Walters, p. 10; Fox (1986), p. 152.

17. Marian Schwab, "Career Lay Ministers," *TODAY'S PARISH* (October 1987): 9–10. Similarly, *National Profile of Diocesan Directors of Religious Education* shows that 44 percent of diocesan directors are men. Joseph Sinwell, Thomas Walters, and Rita Walters (Washington, D.C.: National Catholic Educational Association, 1989).

18. Murnion, p. 27.

19. Fox, p. 201.

20. *No Turning Back* (Chicago: National Association for Lay Ministry, 1996), pp. 32–34.

21. Barbara Castellano, NALM, identified this issue in the consultation process.

22. Murnion, p. 27.

23. Anne Munley, *Threads for the Loom: LCWR Planning and Ministry Studies* (Silver Spring, Md.: Leadership Conference of Women Religious, 1992), pp. 123, 193–4.

24. Murnion, p. 27.

25. Zeni Fox, "Research Report on Youth Ministers" in *Vision and Challenge* (February 1994): 15. Research included laity and vowed religious employed in parishes.

26. Barbara J. Fleischer, *Ministers of the Future: A Study of Graduate Ministry Students in Catholic Colleges and Universities* (New Orleans: Loyola Institute for Ministry, 1993), p. 11. Vowed religious and laity are included.

27. Richard Schoenherr and Lawrence Young, *Full Pews and Empty Altars: The Demographics of the Priest Shortage* (Madison: University of Wisconsin Press, 1993), p. 62.

28. Murnion, p. 27.

29. Fleisher, p. 12.

30. Suzanne Elsesser and Eugene Hemrick, *Preparing Laity for Ministry,* unpublished report, United States Catholic Conference, 1986, p.17.

31. Fr. Allan Figueroa Deck, SJ (National Catholic Council for Hispanic Ministry) and Jacqueline Wilson (Office of Black Catholics) pointed this out in the consultation process.

32. Annette Kane, National Council of Catholic Women, raised this concern in the consultation process.

33. Murnion, pp. 37, 40, 41.

34. Walters (1983), pp. 34–36.

35. Fox (1986), pp. 216–217.

36. Fox (1993), p. 38.

37. Fox (1986,) pp. 217–218.

38. Ibid., pp. 198–199.

39. Murnion, pp. 31–32.

40. Ibid., pp. 33–34.

41. Fox (1993), pp. 12–13.

42. Fox (1986), pp. 161–162.

43. Elsesser and Hemrick, pp. 1 and 9.

44. Charles Topper, Geri Telepak, Thomas Walters and Rita Tyson Walters, *A Survey of Graduate Programs in Ministry 1992–1993* (West Hartford, Conn.: Association of Graduate Programs in Ministry, 1993), pp 63, 65.

45. Report No. 4 (Notre Dame: University of Notre Dame, June 1985), p. 6.

46. Report No. 8 (Notre Dame: University of Notre Dame, July 1986), p. 7.

47. Report No. 14 (Notre Dame: University of Notre Dame, March 1989), p. 4.

48. Ann Patrick Conrad and Joseph J. Shields, *Career Lay Ministers in the Archdiocese of Baltimore: An Assessment of Future Roles and Functions* (Washington, D.C.: Center for Applied Research in the Apostolate, 1982); Dean Hoge, *The Future of Catholic Leadership* (Kansas City, Mo.: Sheed and Ward, 1987); Dean Hoge, "Attitudes of Priests, Adults and College Students on Catholic Parish Life and Leadership," unpublished paper, January 1986.

49. Fox (1986), pp. 208–210.

50. Peter Gilmour, *The Emerging Pastor* (Kansas City, Mo.: Sheed and Ward, 1986). See also, Gary Burkart, *The Parish Life Co-ordinator* (Kansas City, Mo.: Sheed and Ward, 1992).

51. Murnion, pp. 83, 91.

52. Fox (1986), pp. 202–203. This theme emerged as important in focus groups convened by NALM. The conclusion of the report states, "Lay ministry is flourishing, but will not continue to flourish if the individual ministers do not feel accepted and recognized in their various capacities—especially by the clergy." David De Lambo, *NALM Listening Sessions* (Chicago: National Association for Lay Ministry, 1995), pp. 51–52.

53. Ibid., p. 188.

54. Ibid., p. 189 and Fox (1994), 18–19.

55. Murnion, p. 93. Among DREs, in 1992, 43 percent earned $21,000 or more, and 16 percent $27,000 or more. *A Hopeful Horizon*, p. 16.

56. 1995–1996 NACPA National Church Staff Compensation Survey (Fort Worth: National Association of Church Business Administration, 1995).

57. Fox (1986), p. 180. It is important to note that this study included part-time and full-time ministers.

58. Murnion, p. 92.

59. O'Hara, p. 12.

60. Fox (1986), p. 195.

61. Murnion, p. 98.

62. Fox (1986), p. 198.

63. Ibid., p. 195. Even among youth ministers, whom Murnion found to be more dissatisfied in their ministry, 79 percent said they would volunteer, and only 2 percent that they would not (Fox [1994], p. 23).

64. Ibid., pp. 195–198.

65. Ibid., p. 211 and Fox (1994), p. 36.

66. Fox (1986), pp. 204, 211–212 and Fox (1994), pp. 31 and 36.

67. Murnion, p. 13.

68. Fox (1986), pp. 228, 237–238, and Fox (1994), p. 17. Murnion's study gives similar results (pp. 74–75).

69. Murnion, pp. 104–108.

70. Fox (1986), p. 239.

71. Ibid., pp. 220–221. Respondents also said that they were more likely to choose "ministry" than when they began their work. Presuming that trend continued, probably even more would choose "ministry" today.

72. "The Future of Ministry," *America* (March 28, 1981): 243.

73. Fox (1986), pp. 222–223.

74. Reverend Virgil Funk, National Pastoral Musicians, reflected on the "difference between clerical appointment and lay hiring; it is more than just a stipend versus a salary. It is the way each holds office."

75. Ibid., pp. 228–229.

76. Ibid., p. 229.

77. Ibid., p. 242.

78. Ibid., p. 236.

Toward a Theology of Ecclesial Lay Ministry
BY JAMES HEFT, SM, PH.D.

This paper outlines multiple sources for developing a theology of ecclesial lay ministry (ELM): the extent of the profound change through which the Church has gone in the latter half of the twentieth century; insights from Scripture for ELM; the patterns of lay participation in ministry at different points in the history of the Church; and the guidance offered by the magisterium. In order to move toward a more adequate theology of ELM, this paper calls for:

1. *a review of developments in ELM within the United States as well as in other countries;*

2. *a reading of the "signs of the times," that is, how ELM flows from the Gospel and builds on what is good in contemporary culture;*

3. *an examination of what magisterial teaching can contribute to the development of ELM;*

4. *a reflection on the resources within our history that shed light on ELM; and then*

5. *a presentation of several insights derived from these steps. The paper concludes with six suggestions to be clarified and refined by the colloquium participants.*

Introduction

This paper has two objectives. First, it examines several factors that need be taken into consideration before we work on developing a theology of ecclesial lay ministry (ELM). Second, it suggests several steps in our reflection together that if taken will help us arrive at a richer theology of the ELM.[1] To describe such factors and to clarify such steps within the prescribed length for this paper is impossible; hence, at times, a rather uneven movement from some specifics to some generalities exists. If we assume that theology is "any scientific, or methodological, attempt to understand and interpret divine revelation mediated through the data of Scripture and tradition,"[2] then we might have good reason to conclude that since we are undertaking a complex and demanding process, we may not yet be in a position to elaborate a fully developed theology of ELM. Yet we can and should make some fresh attempts to work at fashioning such a theology, especially given the growing importance of ELM in the Church in the United States, as has been described in Zeni Fox's paper.

At the outset of this paper, a clarification needs to be made between what is understood by lay ministry in general and ecclesial lay ministry in particular. The U.S. bishops' document *Called and Gifted for the Third Millennium* gives us their most recent reflections on this distinction. The document itself is divided into four sections: the Call to Holiness, to Community, to Mission and Ministry, and to Christian Maturity. The third section distinguishes between what every Christian is to do and what some who are in the service of the Church are to do.

The U.S. bishops describe the broad understanding of lay ministry when they cite *Christifideles Laici* no. 20 ("Through the sacraments of baptism, confirmation, and Eucharist, every Christian is called to participate actively and co-responsibly in the Church's mission of salvation in the world. Moreover, in those same sacraments, the Holy Spirit pours out gifts which make it possible for every Christian man and woman to assume different ministries and forms of service that complement one another and are for the good of all.") and no. 23 ("Everyone has a responsibility to answer the call to mission and to develop the gifts she or he has been given by sharing them in the family, the workplace, the civic community, and the parish or diocese. A parallel responsibility exists within the Church's leadership 'to acknowledge and foster the ministries, the offices, and the roles of the lay faithful that find their foundation in the sacraments of baptism and confirmation, indeed, for a good many of them in the sacrament of matrimony.'") The bishops underscore, by citing *Christifideles Laici* no. 23 again, *Lumen Gentium* no. 33, and *Familiaris Consortio* no. 53, the responsibility laity have to make the Church present in their families and in secular society, and the responsibility of the parish to "help its members make the connections between worship and work, between liturgy and life in the family, community, and workplace."[3] In these ways, and through these quotations, the U.S. bishops describe lay ministry in general.

Then the bishops turn their attention to ecclesial lay ministers, those who are "professionally prepared lay men and women offering their talents and charisms in the service of the Church."[4] These services include various roles in the celebration of the liturgy (e.g., cantors and music directors, readers and eucharistic ministers, and altar servers), and also "leading Sunday worship" and providing "daily pastoral leadership of a parish" in the absence of a priest or resident pastor. Finally, they list a variety of other ministries (e.g., peace and justice networks, marriage preparation, and some beyond parishes such as in colleges and school systems and social services) and add that when these ministries are "performed in the name of Jesus and enacted under the aegis of the Church," then they are "forms of ministry." Ecclesial lay ministers, the bishops add, think of their work "as a calling," and "often the parish priest is the means of discerning the call."[5] As we shall see, there is not full agreement on precisely what should be included in ELM, and what should be seen as part of lay ministry broadly conceived. We will return to this matter of definition later.

In achieving the two purposes of this paper—looking at sources for a theology of ELM and then delineating steps to be taken in order to sharpen our theological understanding of that new reality in the Church—we will first recall that we are in a period of extensive and rapid change, then explore briefly three important sources for our theological reflection (the reality of lay ministry, the Scriptures, and history); then review the guidance we have to date from the papal, conciliar, and episcopal magisteria; and finally suggest several steps we could take at the colloquium that should help us develop a richer theology of ELM.

PART I: A TIME OF MAJOR TRANSITION

By now, most of us have grown accustomed to hearing that we are in the midst of a major transition in the life of the Catholic Church. The late Karl Rahner pointed out that there are three great epochs in the history of the Church, and that the third was only just beginning in the thinking and practice that constituted the Second Vatican Council. Now, after 1,500 years in its second epoch, the Catholic Church has been leaving behind its predominantly Latin and European shape and sensibility as it struggles to enter many forms as a true world Church.[6] The Second Vatican Council opened the Church to a variety of new influences that have effected a rethinking of liturgical worship; of the relationship between the laity and the clergy, the bishops and the pope; and of the relationship of the Catholic Church to other Christian Churches, to other religions, and indeed, even to those who do not believe. And in the United States, as well as in some other countries, various forms of lay ministry have taken root and enjoyed extensive growth. All of these changes have affected our sense of who we are as a Church, renewed the sense of the Gospel and community among us, and raised some challenging questions.

In the midst of such profound rethinking of the nature of the Church and Christian discipleship, it should not be surprising that there is a call for greater clarity, particularly in those matters where there is very rapid change (e.g., in the forms of religious life), or considerable conflict (e.g., in various types of liberation theology), or even continual tensions (e.g., with delineating the differing roles, rights, and responsibilities of the clergy and laity). We all experience an inherent drive to understand more clearly what we experience and what we are to do. The wise seek only that degree of clarity that actually can be had. In the midst of a period of great change, we need to avoid two equal dangers: forgetting the basic continuities of the Christian life or expecting infallible statements about every pastoral challenge we face.

Turning to the Sources—Key Source: Lay Leadership Today

One key assumption of this paper is that, in this time of great transition, we need in our effort to clarify the theological dimensions of ELM to strike a balance between what we must affirm and what remains open to change. That balance can be struck by articulating more clearly the fundamental theological principles that should frame our considerations about ELM, as well as discerning the legitimate new forms it has and might take. But before such an articulation can be made, we need to review rapidly several critically important sources. Catholic theology has typically turned to Scripture, history, experience, theological reflection, and the official teaching of the magisterium. Vatican II spoke several times of the importance of carefully attending to contemporary developments in culture and understanding them in the light of the Gospel. Reading the "signs of the times" becomes especially challenging when there is relatively new and rapid development.

The development of ELM has been both recent and very rapid in the United States. As a consequence, there is a great need to listen carefully to the experience of those who are in ELM, and who work closely with those in ELM. Again, Zeni Fox's paper provides us with a succinct summary of what we know about ELM. Now we need to identify the most important elements in the experience of ecclesial lay ministers and in the growth and development of ELM. Not insignificant are the sheer numbers of those in ELM: in 1992, 20,000 lay ministers were employed in the United States; and, even more striking, more than 20,000 more are *currently* studying to prepare for lay ministry.[7] When asked, these people stress that bishops ought to be "open to what is happening" and to "avoid foregone conclusions" and not to do "damage to what is already happening." And further, "credibility of the Church is a key issue and it is pretty low, especially among women right now," said some of them. Finally, one representative said, "People want to be heard." Without assuming that these comments represent the thinking of all ministers in the United States, there is a concern, at least among some of them, that their experience needs to be taken seriously by any of us who would want to theologize about ELM. A genuine dialogue with the laity about these matters is especially important for us now.

Also contributing to our understanding of lay ministry today are the results of the Murnion survey, which lists six themes that are especially strong in the development of parish ministry:
1. a shift to a strong lay dimension with attendant change in sensibility;
2. the addition of a strong feminine dimension;
3. a sharp local quality, with all its pluses and minuses (much dependent on local pastor);
4. ministering now done by people with specific professional certification, not necessarily by a distinct category of person such as a vowed or ordained person vs. a lay person;

5. the gradual adoption by parishes and dioceses of personnel policies and practices to ensure just and adequate treatment; and

6. a very low number, proportionately, of Hispanic and African American lay ministers.

These themes reveal a difference not only in the number of ecclesial lay ministers, but in the sensibility they bring to the overall quality of the parish's ministry. What is this difference in sensibility? How significant is it theologically? Since the local pastor is more and more frequently the only priest in the parish, the amount of collaboration between him and the lay ministers has had to grow dramatically. The role of the priest, as one historian put it, has changed from that of an ombudsman to that of an orchestra leader.[8] Unfortunately, historical studies of lay ministry in twentieth-century Catholicism in the United States are as "rare as the bald eagle."[9] The four historical studies that comprise the book entitled *Transforming Parish Ministry: The Changing Roles of Catholic Clergy, Laity, and Women* make clear the extent to which the roles of priest and laity in the United States have changed over the past 100 years. Today, there has to be much more collaboration in the typical parish. Along with greater collaboration, there is also less clarity about distinction in roles. Finally, there is not only a change in sensibility and a need for greater collaboration[10] but also many well-educated women who participate in lay ministries, some of whom continue to experience what they describe as clericalism and a lack of openness on the part of the hierarchy to their perception of the direction the Spirit is taking in the Church today.[11] To the extent that we can genuinely and openly discuss the possibilities and tensions that exist related to women in ministry, we will be able to make a contribution to the further development of a theology of ecclesial lay ministry for the third millennium. Pope John Paul II's letter *Mulieris Dignitatem*, along with other official teachings on the dignity of every baptized person, will be important here.

In an historical essay on lay ministry, Debra Campbell traces the growth of lay involvement in various forms of Christian service, a growth that began in the late nineteenth century, grew stronger in the twenties and thirties during the pontificate of Pius XI, the pope of "Catholic Action," and continued after the Second World War through a variety of developments, including the growth of CCD and CYO, the CFM and Cana movements. By the sixties, when these developments included also Marriage Encounter, Cursillo, and the Charismatic renewal, three fundamental questions about lay activity became clearer:

- What is the proper arena for the activism of the lay apostle: the Church or the world?
- Is there an inherent difference between the vocation of the priest and the vocation of the lay person?
- And finally, can the structures of the institutional Church, including the parish and the diocese, be adapted to accommodate the "emerging" laity, or should alternatives be explored?[12]

This growth of lay involvement in spreading the Gospel and strengthening Christian life preceded the rapid growth of ecclesial lay ministry that we have witnessed during the last three decades. The research done on ecclesial lay ministers indicates that most of them believe that their authority has been delegated to them, and that such an understanding of their role has been accepted not only by the people whom they serve but also by other professional lay staff members. At the same time, there is clear "congregationalist" direction among ecclesial lay ministers in that they seek evaluation not first from their pastor and even less from the bishop and diocesan office, but from the people they serve.[13] Are there some patterns in recent church life and church ministry that are positive and build up the Church? Are some patterns negative or at least a matter of concern? What light might be shed on them, particularly on the matter of the exercise of shared authority? What does a careful reading of canon law tell us about the forms that shared authority might assume between pastors and ecclesial lay ministers? [A paper on canon law and ELM is included later in this volume.] What about the themes underscored in the Murnion research and in the various surveys and dialogues that have taken place? It is extremely important that we take the time to understand as well as we can what has been happening, what in these developments in lay ministry appears on a first reading to build up the life and mission of the Church, and what seems more questionable in what has been happening.

Key Source: The Scriptures

Were we to summarize in brief the most important insights that the Scriptures offer with regard to ELM, they would include the universal call to holiness, a diversity of gifts and a distinction of roles but a unity in the Spirit, ministry as service, and a commissioning for the work of evangelization. These themes receive rich development. In examining these themes, various authors have come to somewhat different conclusions about ministry, and especially about concrete ministries. This should not be surprising, since, as Thomas O'Meara says concerning ministry as described in the New Testament, "from the churches of the first century we have only pieces of a mosaic," even though we do know that after A.D. 100. the three Greek words *Diakonos, presbyter,* and *episkopos* were in place and "survived as permanent basic ministries."[14]

The outline of ministerial activities found in the New Testament reflects a dynamism and a creativity, as well as the need for a certain order and coordination. One only needs to read Paul's letters to the Corinthians to see people with a great diversity of gifts and the challenge these gifted people created for the leadership of the local church community, which was constantly at risk of splintering into factions. This dynamism and creativity ought to be understood as ongoing. The forms that ministries have taken are both culturally attuned and conditioned. Against such a dynamic backdrop, various ministries have been created in response to special needs that arise in the midst of the community. [A paper that treats in greater detail what the Scriptures have to tell us about the ministry of the People of God is included in this volume.] It will be important for us to keep in mind the insights we can cull from the New Testament about ministry, for the history of the Church in regard to the development of ministries is not simply one of continual progress, because for long periods of time certain ministries have disappeared. What is more, for many centuries the only spirituality discussed was typically that of the celibate priesthood.[15]

Key Source: Some Lessons from History

Many examples from history that shed light on patterns of lay participation in ministry could be adduced at this point. We shall limit ourselves to four: the Middle Ages, the Reformation, some examples from the nineteenth century in the United States, and some of the ramifications of Vatican II. The first three examples pertain to the broader understanding of lay ministry in the Church but form an important context for our reflection on ELM. The fourth relates more directly to ELM.

From the fourth and fifth centuries onward, various ministerial roles that had been exercised by the baptized were subsumed into the clerical state, through the Roman *curus clericalis*. These included the ministry of reader, acolyte, and porter, as well as the ministry of widows and deaconesses. Not only did these ministries exist in the Church, but they were recognized by description in church orders and by official installation, such as that found in the *Apostolic Tradition* and the *Apostolic Constitutions*. Beginning with the initiative of Paul VI in *Ministeria Quaedam*, there has been a move to retrieve such ministries as well as their liturgical blessing.[16]

Though such ministries had disappeared, in the evangelical awakening of the eleventh century, lay persons played a considerable part in fostering the renewed following of Jesus Christ and in preaching the Gospel. Pope Gregory IX both restrained and allowed some lay exercise of the word by distinguishing between preaching the Gospel, reserved to priests, and moral or spiritual exhortation. Women also, such as Gertrude of Helfta and Hildegard of Bingen, gave spiritual conferences, which they saw as in some sense a priestly office confided to them by Christ but without the official sanction of being ordained.

From the thirteenth to the fifteenth centuries, considerable ministry was exercised in the Church through the work of confraternities. Their members exercised the service of care of the dying, burial of the dead, care of the bereaved, and other works of mercy. The new forms of devotion to Christ Crucified, to the Blessed Sacrament and to the Virgin Mother of God, owed much to lay initiative and to the public or private devotional exercises of the confraternities.

The Counter Reformation emphasized the ordained priesthood at the expense of the baptismal priesthood of all the faithful. Traditional Catholic theology had taught that every Christian participates by baptism in the priestly, prophetic, and kingly ministry of Christ. Nevertheless, it is now clear in retrospect that one of the prices paid for the Counter Reformation by later generations has been a loss on the part of many laity of a sense of their baptismal priesthood and their responsibility for ministry. Moreover, the fact that most of the laity until this century lacked formal education made it all the easier to load onto the priest all the responsibilities for leadership, including not only those in the sacramental and biblical realms but also, at times, those in the political. The diminishment of the role of the laity persisted, with some notable exceptions,[17] right up until the Second Vatican Council.

A second example comes from the nineteenth-century experience in the United States of trusteeism. Patrick Carey has done the major work on this controversy, which reached its most intense phase before the 1830s. In essence, it represented an attempt to redefine the roles of the laity and of the ordained. Those Catholics who had immigrated to the United States at the beginning of the nineteenth century brought with them from Europe various patronage practices, which, when they were translated into American culture, inevitably "democratized" local parishes and manifested themselves in the desire of the laity to appoint and fire pastors, and not only to manage parish finances and various ecclesiastical affairs but also to own ecclesiastical property.[18] The reaction of the bishops was clear and strong. They affirmed that the locus of all ecclesiastical authority—executive, legislative, and judicial—was the bishop. Peter R. Kenrick, who later became the archbishop of St. Louis, stated that "a bishop should not reason with his flock, but authoritatively direct them."[19] The First Baltimore Council, in 1829, addressed the problem of trusteeism directly, and, in the opinion of Carey, became "the most important single event in marking the decline of clerical and lay influence and in signaling the beginning of the growth of exclusive episcopal power in the government and management of the Church."[20] And even though some of the "republican" bishops, such as John Carroll and John England, consulted trustees and in some cases felt the need to acquire their consent on some temporal matters, they nonetheless did not hold themselves bound to the advice or the consent they would receive from the trustees. Throughout this conflict, as in so many other conflicts in the history of the Church, "[T]he anti-trustees and their opponents rarely made careful theological or even canonical distinctions between the sacrament of orders, canonical mission (or institution) and presentation, election, and nomination and therefore laid themselves open to the charge of confusing doctrine and discipline."[21] As we work through some of the tensions and possibilities in ELM, we need to be attentive to distinctions that will deepen collaboration and strengthen both ordained and lay ministries.

The last example underscores the uniqueness of the question that this colloquium addresses. The question draws upon the traditional distinction between the secular role of the laity and the ecclesial role of the clergy and religious. In the document that resulted from the Synod on the Laity, *Christifideles Laici* (1988), John Paul II issued a warning to the laity in the form of two temptations that must be avoided. In paragraph 2 he states that

> . . . *the synod has pointed out that the post-conciliar path of the lay faithful has not been without its difficulties and dangers. In particular, two temptations can be cited which they have not always known how to avoid: the temptation of being so strongly interested in Church services and tasks that some fail to become actively engaged in their responsibilities in the professional, social, cultural and political world; and the temptation of legitimizing the unwarranted separation of faith from life, that is, a separation of the Gospel's acceptance from the actual living of the Gospel in various situations in the world.*

These needs to sustain a social vision for the Gospel and to avoid privatizing the faith are not simply post-Vatican II challenges. In 1956, for example, John Cogley, once a member of Dorothy Day's Catholic Worker movement and then a writer for *Commonweal*, the lay journal of Catholic opinion, complained about a basic shift in the lay "apostolate," as it was called then, "from social movements to family movements, from the house of hospitality in the slums to the ranch-style house in the suburbs."[22] While a distinction ought to be made between clergy and laity, the line between the Church and the world runs through every Christian's life, ordained or unordained. Karl Barth once said that the minister of the word should have a Bible in one hand and the newspaper in the other. We need to ask then how we can keep both the Church and the world, family movements and social movements, within the vision of all forms of ministry.

The new situation we face, and the one this colloquium addresses, has to do then not with the ministry of lay people broadly understood, but with the ministry of lay professionals within the Church. We are to reflect upon the theological status of these lay people who feel called to work as professionals for the Church, typically within the parish setting. Questions about social commitment and the evangelization of culture are not unique for ecclesial lay ministers, for such challenges confront all the baptized—be they lay or ordained, be they involved in ministry broadly understood or in ELM. We need rather to focus on, for example, the relationship between the ecclesial lay ministers, on the one hand, and the clergy and rest of the laity on the other. We need to understand not only the authority ecclesial lay ministers can and should exercise but also how that authority is granted, and by whom.

The Guidance of the Magisterium
Although a case can be made from New Testament texts—beginning with the writings and example of the apostle Paul—that ministry in and from the Church is not to be the responsibility only—or even primarily—of those who are ordained, the facts of subsequent history indicate that lay ministry has not been a priority of official church teaching until our own century. Already with Pius X (1903–1914), whose motto was "the restoration of all things in Christ," we have a call for cooperation between the clergy and the laity.[23] Pius XI (1922–1939) made the call for lay involvement in the apostolate a key dimension of his pontifical teaching, announcing that call in his first encyclical, *Ubi arcano* (1922). He supported a growing "apostolic spirit" among the laity who participated in the work of bishops and clergy. It is from him that we have the phrase "Catholic Action," defined as "the participation of the laity in the apostolate of the hierarchy." By defining Catholic Action in this manner, the pope made it possible to think that the laity derived their apostolic role not from baptism but from those who were ordained; moreover, he also implied, as Thomas O'Meara points out, that ministry for the laity had come "to the bishops through a historical line

with the Twelve," thereby overlooking the roles of the Spirit and the community.[24] Despite these limitations of the definition of Catholic Action, Pius XI was aware that the laity, "thanks to their very condition, can sometimes accomplish things which are impossible to the clergy, however willing these might be."[25]

The beginnings of the liturgical renewal, the fostering of biblical studies, the development of a theology of the mystical body, and the call for lay missionaries in the 1950s, all helped to pave the way for the Second Vatican Council, which constituted a veritable watershed in thinking about ministry. Suffice it here to recall that the ecclesiology of *Lumen Gentium* highlighted the centrality of the "People of God," developed in a chapter that precedes the chapter that developed the hierarchical structure of the Church. Also highly significant was *Gaudium et Spes*, which called for a positive involvement of all the members of the Church in the transformation of the world. The Church's first official conciliar statement on the apostolate of the laity, *Apostolicam Actuositatem*, made it clear that the Council was committed to recognizing, as it had never done before, the indispensability of "lay ministry" (though the Council did not use these words in this context) in the world. Besides this new emphasis on the role of the laity in the life of the Church, Vatican II also avoided locating the source of all ministry in the hierarchy, and instead "reestablished diversity within traditional Church offices."[26]

The next step taken by the papal magisterium in 1972 when Paul VI (1963–1978) issued *Quaedam* and *Ad Pascendum*, which suppressed the orders of porter and exorcist, retained the orders of reader and liturgical server (acolyte)—both of which were separated from major orders—and opened these to men who by baptism shared in the ministry of Christ. Baptized men could enter these ministries through an installation ceremony that, however, was declared no longer to be an ordination. David Power observed that more important than these documents we have just cited is the realization that during this time, the Church was working hard to keep up with the rapidly developing phenomenon of lay ministry in the Church. Behind these documents, a powerful movement was pushing ecclesial structures to adjust.[27]

In 1987, the Synod of Bishops dealt with the laity. We have already cited this document, *Christifideles Laici*, several times, as do certain paragraphs of the final two documents that we shall now mention. Both come from the U.S. Catholic bishops. The first, *Called and Gifted*, was published in 1980 to mark the fifteenth anniversary of Vatican II's document on the apostolate of the laity. It was organized around four "calls": to holiness, to community, to mission and ministry, and to adulthood/Christian maturity; these four calls, as we noted earlier, were updated in the bishops' 1995 statement *Called and Gifted for the Third Millennium*. In their 1995 statement, the bishops realized that in 1980 they were "just beginning to experience the tide of professionally prepared lay men and women offering their talents and charisms in the service of the Church."[28] They admit that they are now challenged to do the following:

1. commit resources to help the laity prepare for church ministry;
2. provide a living wage;
3. incorporate minority lay ministers into leadership;
4. pray for vocations to priesthood, religious life, *and* lay ministry;
5. work for the common good in society; and, as mentioned earlier,
6. work at ensuring a greater harmony among the increasing diversity of ministries.[29]

PART II: STEPS TO BE TAKEN IN WORKING TOWARD A MORE ADEQUATE THEOLOGY OF ECCLESIAL LAY MINISTRY

It should be clear by now that the question for the colloquium is, How do we construct a more adequate theology of ecclesial lay ministry, so named by the U.S. bishops in their *Called and Gifted for the Third Millennium*?[30] We must focus, then, on the reality of this form of ministry, that is, of the participation in service to the community as such by some of the baptized, as distinguished from the participation in mission that is given by baptism to all the baptized. We need to understand more fully what is meant by saying that actions are ecclesial ministry when done "in the name of Jesus and under the aegis of the Church." Does, for example, reference to "professionals" have some theological import, or is it intended only as a further description of the actual reality of what is occurring in the United States? Theological reflection on these matters should lead to a growth in understanding the phenomenon of ecclesial lay ministry and its relation to the Christian tradition. Such reflection also requires discernment and has as one of its purposes the guiding of practice. What steps can guide us through this process of theological reflection? The following steps are suggested.

Step One: What Is Happening Elsewhere in the Church

Before we plunge fully into the U.S. development, it would be wise to review what has been happening to ELM in the Church on other continents. Such an examination of the experience of the universal Church will allow us to see how ELM partakes of a larger phenomenon and what is distinctive of it in itself. In fact, lay participation in the service, guidance, and leadership of local communities was widespread on other continents before it became so significant on the North American continent.

We have already made reference to some developments in Latin America, where in March 1996 the bishops grouped New Testament texts that shed light on lay ministry into four major groups:
1. the service of the word, which receives the highest priority in the New Testament;
2. the service of charity, which fosters unity and attends to the needy;
3. the service of the liturgy, which includes preaching the Gospel, the saying of prayers, hymns, liturgical assemblies, the ministry of baptism, the eucharistic supper, and the ministry of reconciliation; and
4. the direction of a community of service.[31]

They also name as their top priority the need to develop a theology of lay ministry (they do not use the title, "ecclesial lay ministry," though they acknowledge the need to define more precisely this reality); state that there are no known ecclesial (magisterial) documents precisely on this matter; warn against a tendency toward the clericalization by some lay ministers; and mention the need to clarify both the relationship between lay ministries and the pastoral action of the rest of the parish, as well as the relationship between the priests and lay ministers.

The African Synod of 1994, in addressing the role of the laity, paid much attention to their place in evangelizing African society and culture by their offices in public life and in the development of the family. There was however some mention in the synodal message and in the post-synodal exhortation of Pope John Paul II to their work in fostering the internal life of church communities. One paragraph of the synodal message,[32] and one of the propositions submitted to the pope,[33] underlined the importance of small communities at the human level, that is, "living or basic ecclesial communities." This was repeated in the papal exhortation.[34] Message, propositions, and post-synodal exhortation all likewise underlined the role that catechists have played (and continue to play) in the past in the formation and leadership of Christian communities.[35]

As far back as 1977, the Federation of Asian Bishops had taken note of the growing importance of lay ministry by sponsoring a colloquium on the subject. While again looking to the role of the baptized in society, the colloquium in its conclusions listed the roles of leadership exercised by laity within the Church:

> Leadership roles in the Christian communities are slowly emerging. Among the more important services and functions that are developing are community leaders, ministers of the Eucharist, prayer leader, catechist, treasurer, social worker, youth leader, educator, facilitator or harmonizer of differences, etc.[36]

Step Two: Reading the "Signs of the Times"

This step relates the phenomenon of ELM to a reading of the "signs of the times," reading them and interpreting them in the light of the Gospel, as this expression occurs in *Gaudium et Spes* (no. 4). This process has been developed further by John Paul II in his discourses on Gospel and culture, when he speaks of letting the Gospel take root in culture and of taking into the life of the Church all that belongs to a culture and is not alien to the Gospel (e.g., *Redemptoris Missio*, no. 52).

Through this step we examine how the development of ELM in North America reflects contemporary culture, how far it reveals essential elements of the apostolic tradition, and how far it incorporates some elements of culture that are not "alien" to the Gospel and can indeed serve its rooting in church life and society. Here, we must discern those negative elements that prevent the spread of the Gospel (e.g., the passive role of the laity in the past or in the present; some tendencies toward fragmentation in the community and between forms of ministry.) We must ask to what extent they are indications of something in the culture and to what extent they may be manifestations of true Christian spirituality, albeit allied to cultural experiences. We must also discern positive elements that foster greater participation in the life of the Church (e.g., the understanding of the human person as participatory in community and in the development of the self in community, the insights that sociology and anthropology have afforded us into the importance of ritual and symbol, and efforts to overcome the gender gap in society and the Church and to reflect more on the role of the ministry of women).

Step Three: Official Church Teaching

This step relates what is understood about the reality of lay ministry and the "signs of the times" to official teaching and relevant theological writings. The contributions of Vatican II in this regard depend greatly on the work of Yves Congar.[37] We have already mentioned the role of Paul VI in developing the liturgical ministry of the baptized and the letters of John Paul II *Christifideles Laici* and *Mulieris Dignitatem*, as well as the new *Code of Canon Law*. Attention to the magisterial teachings helps us to see where the development of ELM fits as an ecclesial reality as well as the questions that ELM raises in regard to this reality.

Of particular relevance are the teachings on the participation in the mystery of Christ and the Spirit and in mission, which comes with baptism, and the foundation of the distinction between a share in mission (witness to the Gospel in the world) and a share in ministry (direct service to the community of faith) in an understanding of how the inner life of the Church and its witness to the Gospel are related. It is in this context that *Lumen Gentium* (no. 31) made a working distinction between the role of the laity, of the ordained, and of religious, even though elsewhere it showed how the baptized have a part in developing the inner life of the Church as well as in its mission to the world.

Step Four: Lessons from History and Tradition

At this point, we reflect on the resources within our history that might shed light directly upon the reality of ELM, which we look at from a new standpoint of experience. Included in our examination in step four are the following: the New Testament ecclesial life and ministry; the growth of the distinction between *kleros* and *laos*, as distinct from the sacrament of orders within community and church life; the evangelical awakening of the eleventh century and the role of confraternities in the following centuries, the Reformation, and the tension between the priesthood by ordination and that by baptism; and the various experiences in the history of the Church in the United States that have shaped our sense of the relationship between priests and laity.

Step Five: Fashioning a Theology of ELM from the Results of the Previous Steps

This step attempts to spell out the insights derived from the process of reflection in which we have been engaged. The following suggestions are offered, but they could be challenged or enlarged in a discussion that draws from the sources studied and reads the "signs of the times":

- Through baptism, all Christians have a share in the mission of Christ and the Spirit.
- One type of service is more directly related to the presence of the Gospel in the world (witness and proclamation); another is more directly related to the service of the inner life of the Church. These two are not to be separated, but the growth and service of church life and community are to be seen in relation to the power of community and of persons to make the Gospel known.
- There is a sense in which ecclesial ministry (contribution to the growth of the life of the Church) belongs to all the baptized, but this has to be related to what John Paul II has called the "catechumenal character" of all Christian life,[38] that is, persons can live the full life of faith and can assume responsibilities only as they grow in the life of Christ and of the Spirit through a process of initiation. In this sense, the call is not simply "given" in baptism, but it is a vocation—one that matures in faith through this process of initiation.

- The Church has to be attentive to the proper relation between a personal call to serve and community needs, in which all ministry and call is rooted.
- Church communion in faith and action always is the primary symbol of the communion of the divine persons and of the presence and action of Christ and Spirit in the world, as it is organically formed (recall the Pauline metaphor of the body). In this perspective of organic communion, the relationship between ministry of the baptized and that of the ordained is an organic one, within a sacramentally differentiated organism. It should be remembered that canonical language and regulation need to be rooted in the living organism and its inner relations.
- Thought also has to be given to the kind of recognition, both institutional and liturgical, that may be given to those called to "ecclesial lay ministry."

Conclusion

This paper has attempted to do two things: to identify a number of sources, both historical and theological, which ought to be examined by anyone who wishes to develop a theology of ELM; and to propose five steps that will guide our approach in this effort. The sources are explored in greater detail by those commissioned to write other papers for the colloquium. At the colloquium, bishops, theologians, and lay ministers engaged in a substantive discussion about all these issues. There is a growing realization in the Church that this rapid growth in ELM should be understood not as a temporary supplement for a diminished number of priests and religious but as a movement of the Spirit that reflects a fuller embodiment of ministry in the Church. Our task is to make clearer the theological basis and dimensions for that fuller embodiment and to offer proposals that will strengthen its contribution to the life of the Church, and finally, in the process, to clarify the place of ELM in the rich panoply of ministries in the Church.

Appendix

Several Specific Issues for Examination at the Colloquium

In this appendix, we will identify three specific issues that emerge from the research on ELM: the description of ministry, the language we use to say what we mean by lay ministry, and the tensions and possibilities inherent in the professionalization of ministry. Each has theological ramifications that need to be addressed through the process outlined in the second part of this paper.

Description

If we are to develop a theology of ELM, we would be helped if we could agree upon a *description* of what it is. In the first part of this essay, dealing with "lay leadership today," we gave some indication of the scope and variety of lay ministries in the Church today. The NCCB Committee on Doctrine reserved the term "ministry" to two specific forms: "ordained ministry," that is, the public work done by bishops, priests, and deacons, and then "designated lay ministry," that is, the ministry carried out by people officially commissioned as lectors or acolytes. All other work by the unordained was called "Christian service."[39]

Thomas O'Meara offers another definition, which, if not narrow, does not name as ministry all the good things a baptized Christian might do. His definitions reads: "Christian ministry is the public activity of a baptized follower of Jesus Christ flowing from the Spirit's charism and an individual personality on behalf of a Christian community to witness to, serve, and realize the kingdom of God."[40] He arrived at this definition only after studying the apostolic Church from which he derives six characteristics that theologically compose the nature of ministry: "ministry is (1) doing something; (2) for the advent of the kingdom; (3) in public; (4) on behalf of a Christian community; (5) which is a gift received in faith, baptism and ordination; and which is (6) an activity with its own limits and identity within a diversity of ministerial actions."[41]

O'Meara argues for this understanding of ministry, for it makes clear, to expand briefly on each of the six points, that a Christian is baptized into a community of (1) service, for a clear purpose of building (2) the kingdom, in a way that (3) "normally takes on a visible and public form in words and deeds" (otherwise, "every noble movement or good deed is ministry," and "when everything is ministry, nothing is ministry"; and conversely, "the public characteristic of ministry challenges any rechanneling of Christian service into liturgy alone or into inner piety"), and (4) flows from the community to build up the kingdom, and is manifest in (5) many forms from the spirit as a (6) plurality of ministries.[42]

O'Meara is not trying to define ELM; rather, he is trying to describe what is the essence of Christian ministry as understood through the apostolic Church.[43] Fearing that the terminology would lessen the ecclesial significance of the mission to the world in testifying to the Gospel, David Power favors a broader use of the word *ministry* that would not prefix some services with the word *ecclesial*. He writes:

> *Ministeriality is a quality of the Church community as a unit or body, before it is a predicate of any of its members. The fundamental principle for an understanding and a structuring of ministry is that the Church is the sacrament of God's kingdom in the world, a living presence which must deal with temporal questions. How the Church sees itself in relation to these questions determines the ministeriality of the community. . . . Today we have to look to the community's experience of Christ and of the kingdom in order to discern the charisms and ministries of the Church.*

Finally, the U.S. bishops in their 1995 statement *Called and Gifted for the Third Millennium*, in a section entitled "Lay Ministry in the Church," speak of those who are "professionally" prepared who offer "their talents and charisms in the service of the Church," and who are "often called ecclesial lay ministers."[44] But in this same short two-page section, they also speak about those who work in soup kitchens and in shelters, who teach in church schools and colleges, and who work in social services and act as health care providers as people who are exercising their "designated ministry."[45] Is there an advantage for us at this point in our history of rapidly developing ministries to try to define precisely what we intend to include and exclude under the term "ecclesial lay ministry"?

Apt and Illuminating Words

People communicate through—and sometimes despite—language. Moreover, language frequently indicates fundamental theological perspectives. For example, the shift from the word *apostolate*, which suggests that the laity participates in the work of the hierarchy, to the word *ministry*, which can flow from both baptism and orders, is a profound shift in and enrichment of ecclesiology. Is there some way, in keeping with the distinction between the hierarchy and the laity, that we can find language that would be less pejorative than "lay" and "laity," at least as these words are used in our culture today? To be a "layman" in some field means to be an amateur. Ministry that is "lay" then becomes, accordingly, associated with the work of amateurs. Of course, it should be recognized that the word clergy frequently evokes a negative connotation as well. What if we were to speak rather of "ministries of the ordained and of the baptized?" Suppose further, if we were to keep with the direction taken by *Called and Gifted for the Third Millennium*, we would speak more specifically of "ecclesial ministries of the baptized." Several focus groups of U.S. bishops indicated a "strong desire for a consistent glossary of terms, e.g., pastoral associate vs. pastoral minister vs. parish administrator vs. pastoral coordinator."[46] The problem with language and consistency of usage has posed challenges, not surprisingly, to other Christian Churches. The Missouri Synod Lutherans, for example, proposed over a decade ago to speak of "Ministers of Religion, Ordained," "Ministers of Religion, Commissioned," and "Certified Church Workers, Lay."[47] Whatever we finally decide to call these various ministries, it is crucial that the language we use not only respect the variety of possible ministries but also indicate clearly that the source of ministry is ultimately the Spirit and the sacraments of baptism and orders. In the last analysis, this issue of proper terminology is not just a matter of greater clarity for pastoral organization; it is also, and even primarily, a matter of theology.

Professionalization

A third specific issue is that of *professionalism*. This topic generates some tension. Again, the recent bishops' focus groups articulated several questions about professionalism:

> *Is the professional minister distinct from the minister called by vocation? Does "professional" simply mean "paid"? How does the "professional" differ from and relate to the volunteer? Is professionalism a new clericalism, based on degree rather than ordination? How will the attention given to professional ministry within the Church affect the call of all the baptized to ministry to the "marketplace"?*[48]

Some bishops mentioned the need to help pastors especially to learn how to collaborate with professionals. And if we strongly support the development of professional lay ministry precisely at the time when the numbers of those accepting calls to the priesthood and religious life continues to drop, will we, asked some, actually continue to drive down the number of priestly and religious vocations? The bishops argued that we need to learn how to encourage and to support strongly religious, priestly, and lay ministries and not put them in competition.

Also a part of this same discussion about the preparation of professional lay ministers is the distrust that some bishops have of lay ministers who have been educated in graduate schools. Can graduate schools discern the "call" to lay ministry? Should they presume to? Or should all such discernment be done rather by bishops and diocesan personnel? Should graduate schools provide in their pastoral and ministerial programs for lay people a strong spiritual component, providing opportunities not just for study but also for prayer and spiritual direction?

Finally, an aspect of professionalism that seems to create some tension is the "strong resistance" by some bishops to "viewing lay ministry as a profession or function, and to discussing or giving priority to professional issues (e.g., portability of benefits, salaries, job security, etc.)," a position that is in "stark contrast to feedback to date from lay ministers where these issues are of paramount importance" (*Bishops' Lay Ministry Focus*

Groups). The Murnion research shows that when asked to rank order the source of their authority, ecclesial lay ministers answered first, with strong preference, baptism and confirmation; second, professional training and competence; and third, a vocation from God.[49] In the 1995 U.S. bishops' document *Called and Gifted for the Third Millennium,* the bishops promise to address these tensions so that more effective professional lay ministry might flourish in the Church. What needs to be done now to make progress in addressing professionalism in ELM?

Notes

1. This paper has benefited from many suggestions made by members of the Theological Steering Committee and especially those made by David N. Power, OMI. Moreover, comments from Michael Barnes, Una Cadegan, Dennis Doyle, M. Therese Lysaught, Maureen and Terry Tilley, and Sandra Yocum Mize—all colleagues at the University of Dayton—steered me consistently in fruitful directions.

2. Gerald O'Collins, *The HarperCollins Encyclopedia of Catholicism*, Richard P. McBrien, ed. (San Francisco, HarperCollins, 1995), 1250.

3. National Conference of Catholic Bishops, *Called and Gifted for the Third Millennium* (Washington, D.C.: United States Catholic Conference, 1995), p. 15.

4. Ibid., p. 16.

5. Ibid., p. 17.

6. "Towards a Fundamental Interpretation of Vatican II," *Theological Studies* 40 (1979): 721 ff.

7. *Lay Ministry Update*, vol. 1, no. 2, March/April 1996.

8. R. Scott Appleby, "Present to the People of God: The Transformation of the Roman Catholic Parish Priesthood," *Transforming Parish Ministry: The Changing Roles of Catholic Clergy, Laity, and Women Religious*, Jay P. Dolan, R. Scott Appleby, Patricia Byrne, and Debra Campbell (New York: The Crossroad Publishing Co., 1989), pp. 13, 83.

9. Jay P. Dolan, "Preface," Ibid., ix.

10. See the 1995 statement of the U.S. Catholic bishops, where it is stated that "The new evangelization will become a reality only if ordained and lay members of Christ's faithful understand their roles and ministries as complementary, and their purposes joined to the one mission and ministry of Jesus Christ" (*Called and Gifted for the Third Millennium*, p. 18).

11. See the article by theologian Catherine Mowry LaCugna, "Catholic Women as Ministers and Theologians," *America* (October 10, 1992), in which she calls for a more focused theological reflection on the significance of gender (p. 239), and sees irony in the exclusion of women from the ordained ministry in the Catholic Church, since that exclusion has been a factor that has led a number of them to pursue doctorates in theology. These women now provide major leadership as Christian feminist thinkers. See also Dolores Leckey's address, "Toward a Partnership of Women and Men in Mission," *Origins* (December 5, 1996): 416–420, which provides a thoughtful reflection upon the complementary ways men and women might recognize each other's insights more readily in their ministerial roles.

12. Debra Campbell, "The Struggle to Serve: From the Lay Apostolate to the Ministry Explosion," *Transforming Parish Ministry*, Jay P. Dolan, R. Scott Appleby, Patricia Byrne, and Debra Campbell (New York: The Crossroad Publishing Co., 1989), p. 254.

13. See Z. Fox paper, pp. 14–15.

14. Thomas Franklin O'Meara, OP, *Theology of Ministry* (Ramsey, N.J.: Paulist Press, 1983), pp. 91–92.

15. Ibid., p. 22.

16. For a study of this, see David N. Power, *Gifts that Differ: Lay Ministries Established and Unestablished* (New York: Pueblo, 2nd edition, 1985), pp. 145–170.

17. See, for example, Patrick Carey's "Lay Catholic Leadership in the United States" in *U.S. Catholic Historian* (Summer 1990): 223–247, and the essay mentioned earlier by Debra Campbell.

18. See Patrick Carey, *People, Priests, and Prelates: Ecclesiastical Democracy and the Tensions of Trusteeism* (Notre Dame, Ind.: University of Notre Dame Press, 1987), p. 287.

19. Ibid., p. 209.

20. Ibid., p. 214.

21. Ibid., p. 213.

22. R. Scott Appleby, *Transforming Parish Ministry*, p. 248. Sometimes, the laity asked for more responsibility in the running of the parish. A 1965 editorial in the *Brooklyn Tablet* asks that the laity be given "responsibilities . . . more agonizing than the annual bazaar and something a little more profound than handling the roll call at the Holy Name meeting" (p. 260). But the sort of responsibilities that the editorial suggests remain church-focused: some influence in planning the times of Masses and confession and in proposing the topics of sermons. One historian goes so far as to describe the shift Cogley spoke of in 1956 as one from "an activist" model of lay ministry to a "therapeutic model" of the Marriage Encounter and Cursillo movements (p. 265).

23. Pope Pius X, *Il fermo proposito* in *The Lay Apostolate* (Boston: St. Paul Editions, 1961), p. 212. Cited by Debra Campbell in *Transforming Pastoral Ministry*, p. 224.

24. O'Meara, *Theology of Ministry*, p. 138.

25. Pope Pius XI, *Ubi arcano* and "Letter to the Piedmontese Bishops" (1926), in *The Lay Apostolate*, 273–75, 279. Cited by Debra Campbell in *Transforming Pastoral Ministry*, p. 224.

26. O'Meara, p. 146. He continues: "First, the Council established a true ministry of deacon open to men from various manners of Christian life. Although the restored diaconate has not escaped difficulties (the deacon can easily become clericalized, and an extra-

liturgical dimension is frequently missing), this restoration is important. In the diaconate today we have a ministry and an ordination which do not lead to priesthood; we have Christians being ordained who are not pledged to celibacy, men who are not members of a quasi-monastic state. Second, conciliar theology located the priesthood as a ministerial representative of the leader of the local Church, the bishop. The original meaning of 'presbyter' was reintroduced and this gave an identity to this ministry which was other than sacral priest or the lowly parish assistant. Finally, Vatican II described the bishop as a proper ministry and not as a dignity added to or a version of priesthood. We now have three separate ministries with three ordinations; no ministry leads to another nor does one by essence encompass the others. The bishop is the minister to whom presbyter and deacon relate as co-workers"(146).

27. David N. Power, *Gifts that Differ: Lay Ministries Established and Unestablished* (New York, 1980), p. 31ff., cited by O'Meara, pp. 147–148.

28. *Called and Gifted for the Third Millennium*, p. 16.

29. See Appendix for more specific problem areas in ELM revealed by recent research.

30. *Called and Gifted for the Third Millennium*, pp. 15–17.

31. *Latin American Meeting on Lay Ministries in the New Evangelization* (Caracas: Venezuela, March 15–17, 1996), 23.

32. *The African Synod, Documents, Reflections, Perspectives.* Complied by African Faith and Justice Network (Maryknoll, NY: Orbis Books, 1996), p. 78.

33. Ibid., p. 90.

34. Ibid. p. 260.

35. Ibid., pp. 84, 91, 261.

36. See "Asia Colloquium on Ministries: Conclusions" *Origins* 8 (1978): 129–143.

37. For a summary of theology of laity before the Council, see David N. Power, *Gifts that Differ: Lay Ministries Established and Unestablished* (New York: Pueblo, 2nd Edition, 1985).

38. Message to the Brazilian Bishops, *Notitiae* 32 (1996/4): 188.

39. This effort by the NCCB Committee on Doctrine to narrow the definition of the word *ministry* was not reflected in John Paul II's text from the Synod on the Family, *Familiaris Consortio*, par. 53, where the pope speaks of the evangelizing role of parents as "ministry."

40. O'Meara, p. 142.

41. Ibid. p. 137.

42. Ibid. pp. 136–142. Another author, John N. Collins, not a Catholic, favors a more narrow definition of ministry. In his study *Diakonia: Reinterpreting the Ancient Sources* (New York, N.Y.: Oxford University Press, 1990), he writes that "the minister's authority is the conviction of faith expressed by those who received the word; the minister's authenticity, on the other hand, is his or her recognition in and by the Church, whether that be by episcopal ordination or some other process" (p. 158). See also his more popular study *Are All Christians Ministers?* (Collegeville, MN: The Liturgical Press, 1992).

43. Not all authors agree that Christian ministry should be defined narrowly; see, for example, Robert J. Hater, who defines ministry as "the participation in the communication of God's love for all people, a love revealed fully in Jesus Christ," an activity coextensive with evangelization, in *Parish Catechetical Ministry* (Encino, Calif.: Benzinger Publishing Co., 1986), pp. 1–2.

44. *Called and Gifted for the Third Millennium*, p. 16.

45. Ibid., p. 17.

46. *Report from the NCCB Subcommittee on Lay Ministry* (June 1995), 3.

47. *Lay Ministry Update*, vol. 1, no. 5, Sept/Oct 1996.

48. *Lay Ministry Update*, vol. 1, no. 4, Jul/Aug 1996.

49. See Z. Fox paper, p. 16.

Baptism and the Baptized in Church Leadership

BY ZOILA L. DIAZ, D. MIN.

The author's theological reflections on the leadership exercised by the baptized are influenced by her twenty years of experience in ministry formation in the Archdiocese of Miami. The baptized have the responsibility and right to work in making the Christian community an effective sign of God's reign in the world. The call to ministry must be discerned by the minister and the community, examining the charism and competence of the minister and the needs of the community. The ministry must be recognized by the community.

The paper suggests five categories of ecclesial lay ministers. In the comments on multiculturalism, percentages of ethnic groups in 1992 and projections for 2050 are included. Statistics for different groups in the Archdiocese or Miami are supplemented by comments on the social and cultural characteristics of the groups. The paper concludes by identifying three issues for exploration by the colloquium: professionalism, discernment/call, and the overwhelmingly Hispanic Church of 2050.

Introduction

The purpose of this paper is to reflect theologically on the leadership roles exercised by the baptized in the Catholic Church in the United States as described by Zeni Fox in her paper. This reflection will be based on the nature of the sacrament of baptism and of the call to ministry, and it will be guided by some post-conciliar documents and authors.

The U.S. Catholic bishops have recently reaffirmed their 1980 definition of *ecclesial lay ministers*. They are those *"professionally prepared lay men and women offering their talents and charisms in the service of the Church."*[1] In an attempt to further clarify this concept and because we think that it better reflects the reality as presented in Zeni Fox's paper, the following quote from the focus description of the *Theological Colloquium on Ecclesial Lay Ministry*, is invaluable to the content of this paper:

> As non-ordained persons ministering in a formal leadership role in the Church, ecclesial lay ministers may be paid or volunteer; they may possess an academic degree from a university or college or have some kind of certification from a formation program; they are serving in a ministerial area . . . which is recognized and supported by the parish community; they are serving in a committed and stable manner which may be specified by a contract or agreement and/or some type of commissioning by the community.[2]

Lastly, this paper is influenced by the author's experience of more than two decades of serving as an ecclesial lay minister in the Catholic Archdiocese of Miami, recruiting, forming, placing, and evaluating Catholic men and women who, for the most part, serve as volunteer leaders within the local ecclesial community.

The Nature of the Sacrament of Baptism

Based on 1 Peter 2:9–10, chapter II of *Lumen Gentium* develops the doctrine of the unity of all members of the Church. In this Church, the entire people of God are "incorporated into the Church through baptism" sharing in the priestly, prophetic, and royal offices of Christ. This unity is prior to all distinctions. The Spirit of God, alive in this Church, distributes gifts to each at will, but those gifts are given for the "renewal and the up-building of the Church." It is the Spirit who distributes "special graces among the faithful of every rank."[3]

The common priesthood of all the faithful is stressed, but even though the distinction can be made between the "common priesthood of all the faithful" and the "ministerial or hierarchical priesthood," the laity, just by being part of this new people of God, are involved in the mission of Christ and his Church.[4] Vatican II tells us that any renewal in the Church is meaningless without the involvement of the lay faithful.[5]

The document on *The Rite of Christian Initiation of Adults* and the new *Catechism of the Catholic Church* offer us two descriptions of baptism that reveal the rights and responsibilities of the baptized. We will begin our exploration of those rights and responsibilities with the following description: "Baptism incorporates us into Christ and forms us into God's people. This first sacrament pardons all our sins, rescues us from the power of darkness, and brings us to the dignity of adopted children . . ."[6]

It incorporates us into Christ: The person baptized belongs to the one who redeemed us by his death and resurrection; belongs no longer to him/herself. The *responsibility* is to submit to others, especially to the Church's leaders and to serve others "in the communion of the Church,"[7] since "baptism gives a share in the common priesthood of all believers."[8] All the People of God share in the priestly, prophetic, and royal offices of Christ and, therefore, are *responsible* for the mission and service that flows from them.

It forms us into God's people: Since baptism incorporates us into the Church, it makes us members of the Body of Christ, members of the "people of God of the New Testament."[9] A people that is beyond any type of differences (ethnic, gender, racial, cultural). A body that is first the People of God and next, revealer of God's unity in diversity .

It pardons all our sins . . . brings us to the dignity of adopted children . . . : The *Catechism of the Catholic Church* presents the two principal effects of baptism: purification from sin and a new birth in the Holy Spirit. "Baptism not only purifies from all sins, but also makes the neophyte 'a new creature,' an adopted child of God who has become a 'partaker of the divine nature,' member of Christ and coheir with him, and a temple of the Holy Spirit."[10]

The baptized becomes a new creature that enjoys rights as well as responsibilities within the Church. Those *rights* are identified: "to receive the sacraments, to be nourished with the Word of God, and to be sustained by the other spiritual helps of the Church."[11] The *responsibilities* are also identified as the following: to belong to Christ and, therefore, to submit to others especially to the church leaders; to serve others in the communion of the Church; to work toward unity in the People of God; and to participate in the apostolic and missionary activity of the Church, within the marketplace.[12]

In summary, those "'reborn as sons of God [the baptized] *must* profess before men the faith they have received from God through the Church' and participate in the apostolic and missionary activity of the People of God."[13]

The picture that emerges from the reading of these documents is that baptism establishes a relationship between God and the individual and among all the baptized by incorporating them into the Christian community. This is the *identity* of the new People of God. Its mission is to be "salt of the earth and light to the world," and its *destiny*, the extension of the reign of God.[14]

From baptism emerge the bases for the lay person's *responsibility* and *right* to work in the making of the Christian community as an effective sign of God's reign in the world. Those bases are
  1. The unity of the faithful is prior to all distinctions;[15]
  2. Ministry is rooted in the Holy Spirit;[16]
  3. The Spirit's gifts are given for the building up of God's reign;[17]
  4. As a result of the baptismal state, it is from the union of the baptized with Christ himself that the call to ministry springs forth.[18]

It is evident that the sacrament of baptism is not an isolated act, but a communal event—an ecclesial happening. A baptized person is, by reason of its identity, irrevocably linked to the community that welcomed her or him.

The Nature of the Call to Ministry
In reflecting on the nature of the call to ministry, we identify the following principles:

It links ministry and community. Vatican II made this principle official teaching of the Church,[19] and the theologians Congar, Power, and Schillebeeckx all agree on this point, but with different gradations.

Congar agrees in a universal fashion. In his 1972 article, he proposed community as the locus for ministries and used this principle as the entering door for his schema:

> *Jesus has instituted a* structured community *which is as an entirety holy, priestly, prophetic, missionary, apostolic; it has* ministries *at the heart of its life, some freely raised up by the Spirit, others linked by the imposition of hands to the institution and mission of the Twelve . . . ministries are placed as* modes of service *of what the community is called to be and do.*[20] *(Emphasis added).*

Power affirms this principle more concretely by saying that we cannot theologize about ministries except in the context of a Christian community:

> *Today, the main fact of the practical order which has similarly to be taken into account is probably that of the grass-roots Christian community, or* comunidad de base. *This teaches us that* we cannot theologize about ministries except in the context of a Christian community *which corporately assumes responsibility for its own community affairs and for the community's mission in the temporal and social area . . .*[21]

In his treatment of the ordained ministry, Schillebeeckx also stresses this link. He states that ministry emerged from "the apostolic building up of the community," and that when one looks at past developments of ministerial forms, one discovers that "on each occasion official documents sanction a Church practice which has grown up from the grass roots."[22]

Ministry and mission are interrelated. All three authors mentioned in this paper agree on this principle. The community founded by the Lord Jesus Christ has a mission that is that of the Lord himself: "I must proclaim the good news of the kingdom of God" (Lk 4:43). The Holy Spirit brings forth gifts and ministries for the building up of the Christian community. Therefore, there is a strong link between community and ministry and, consequently, between ministry and the Christian community's mission to build up the reign of God in both the spiritual and material realms.[23]

Power emphasizes that lay ministries flourish in a community that is endowed with a sense of mutual service and mission. He stresses that it is in this environment that the question of lay ministries arises. This is contrary to the old Catholic Action position that saw lay ministries (apostolate) as springing "from a concern merely to increase the number of those willing to help presbyters and bishops in their tasks."[24]

A ministry is discerned. If there is a strong link between the Christian community and ministry, then the call to ministry has to be discerned, both by the minister and by the community. Because of the central connection between the baptized and the community that welcomed them, the idea of a minister who goes through a discernment process that ignores the role of the community, is a contradiction.

Reflecting on the concept of vocation in the light of his 1972 schema, Congar told us that while during early Christianity the community elected one of its members to be consecrated either a presbyter or a bishop without even consulting him, today we experience the reverse. We respect the freedom of the minister, but the community is not consulted. Congar stresses that "the exact nature of vocation to the ministry involves the link between ministry and community."[25]

In the process of discerning a call to ministry two elements have to be carefully examined:
1. the minister has to have the *charism(s)* and the *competence* for the ministry, and
2. the community has to have the *need* for such ministry. Power tells us that, "the proper place for discernment and approval of ministries is within local or particular communities of the baptized."[26]

The first three points lead into the principle that **ministry has to be recognized by the Christian community.** For a ministry to be legitimate, it needs some sort of validation or recognition by the community. Schillebeeckx tells us that "The recognition of someone as a minister by the Church (people and leaders) is decisive."[27] There is less clarity as to the mode that this recognition takes.

In treating the question of how lay ministers may be commissioned and/or blessed, we already learned that Power sees the Christian community as the locus for the question of lay ministries. But he adds that taking community as the proper milieu to deal with a theology of ministries and their recognition "is not to reduce ministry to a call from the community." On the contrary, ministry also has a personal dimension since it is performed by the individual bearing the mark of the gift of the Holy Spirit received at baptism. Yet, as a member of the Body of Christ, the person "is enabled to contribute to the life and mission of the community when the gift is virtually or formally recognized by the community."[28]

In brief, the call to ministry cannot be considered outside of the realms of the community of the baptized and of its mission. It is precisely this strong connection that brings up the need for the call to ministry to be both discerned and recognized in order for it to be legitimate.

THE EXPERIENCE OF ECCLESIAL LAY MINISTRY IN THE CHURCH IN THE UNITED STATES

Zeni Fox's Paper

Zeni Fox's paper reflects accurately the current situation of ecclesial lay ministry (ELM) in the United States. The baptized are definitely exercising leadership roles in the parish, in the diocese, and in the Catholic institutions. The following five points are elements of the present reality.

1. **Defining the population:** Although ELM is flourishing[29] in the Church in the United States, the current research uses different and, at times, seemingly contradictory standards for the definition of this population. Norms such as an employee (full and part time) or a volunteer, vowed religious or lay, leader or participant in a ministry, and possessing some kind of credential (academic degree or certification)[30] may be among the reasons for the lack of clarity in defining the ELM population.

In addition, the ecclesial lay ministers reported that they would like to see their role and function clarified.[31] A possible outcome of the colloquium may be a clearer definition of our targeted population.

2. **Leadership Roles Exercised by the ELM:** The leadership roles that the baptized are exercising in the parish, diocese, and/or Catholic institutions[32] could be grouped in five broad areas:[33]

   - *Christian Education Ministries:* This area comprises educational ministers such as presidents, deans, principals, elementary teachers, and college and seminary professors. It also includes religious education ministers such as DREs, RCIA coordinators, and catechists among others.
   - *Evangelization:* Embraces outreach coordinators and workers.[34]
   - *Liturgical Ministries:* It includes directors of liturgy, liturgists, music ministers, ministers of the eucharist, lectors, acolytes, prayer leaders, and ministers of liturgical art and architecture.
   - *Pastoral Ministries:* This broad area contains pastoral care ministers to the sick, the disabled, the elderly, and the dying. It also encompasses ministers to family, to youth and young adults, to migrants and refugees, to special populations and detention ministers, to directors of social concerns, to campus ministers, and to chaplains.
   - *Organizational Ministries:* These ministries deal with the organizational needs of parishes, dioceses, and institutions and include parish administrators or directors, chancellors, superintendents of schools, chief administrator officers, and directors and staff of diocesan offices. It also encompasses pastoral assistants and coordinators of lay ministries.

   This list is not intended to be exhaustive, but it reflects a diversity of ministries performed by the thousands of employed and volunteer laity and vowed religious who are exercising formal leadership roles previously held by clergy. The findings may be pointing in the direction of a more encompassing concept of ecclesial lay ministry that may include both employed and volunteer service.[35]

3. **ELM Role in Forming Christian Community:** In Zeni Fox's paper, we learn that parish ministers contribute significantly to parish life

and that they are perceived by others as serving the formation of the Christian community.[36] But not only are they perceived by others as serving the formation of the community; in another study, the lay ministers themselves ranked "community builder" as the most important function of their work.[37]

It is evident that the ecclesial lay ministers influence the formation of Christian community by serving in the most valued areas of church life with a conscious effort toward community building.

4. **Processes of discernment, choice, and/or appointment for ELM:** Except for the role of councils, Zeni Fox does not report the existence of formal processes of discernment among the respondents to the various studies examined in her paper. But Fox does report that "the great majority of lay ministers (87%) have taken part in a nondegree program related to their ministry," and that "twice as much time is given to spiritual formation of participants in nondegree programs as in degree programs."[38]

Basic elements of a formal discernment process are also reported: (a) sense of call (vocation); (b) giftedness; (c) competence; (d) needs to be addressed; (e) models in the community; (f) the role of the community in the process; and (g) the relationship with the ecclesial authority.[39]

The profile that emerges is of lay persons who are more likely to have gone through a formal process of discernment of ministry if they graduated from a nondegree program rather than from an academic program.

5. **Commissioning/Installation:** The only official rite of installation that exists was given to us in 1972 by Pope Paul VI in *Ministeria Quaedam*.[40] Fox reported that only 7 percent were said to have a formal commissioning service. At the same time, 40 percent said yes, and 34 percent perhaps, when asked if they would choose "a rite of installation in their roles, if there were one." In addition, those who saw their work in the Church as a permanent commitment would choose a rite of installation.[41]

Multiculturalism

The Roman Catholic Church in the United States is multicultural and multiethnic. The 1994 *Official Catholic Directory* lists the U.S. Catholic population at more than 58 million, or more than 23 percent of the total population.[42] This total population reached 255 million in 1992, as a mosaic of diverse cultural and ethnic groups: non-Hispanic white, 75 percent; Asian and Pacific Islander, 3 percent; Hispanic, who may be of any race, 9 percent; African American, 12 percent; and American Indian, Eskimo, and Aleut, 0.8 percent.[43] It is projected that by the year 2050, the non-Hispanic white population will decrease to 53 percent, while minority groups such as American Indian-Eskimo-Aleut, Asian-Pacific Islander, African American, and Hispanic will increase respectively to 1.2, 11, 16, and 21 percents of the total population.[44]

While the Asian population is the fastest growing race group in the United States, the Hispanic growth rate is five times that of non-Hispanics. In addition, the *Catholic Almanac* shows that 80 percent of U.S. Hispanics are Catholic.[45] "By the second decade of the next century, the Church in the United States will very likely be more than 50 percent Hispanic."[46] These figures raise some questions about the results, confirmed by other studies, of the *New Parish Ministries* in which 95 percent of the new ministers are non-Hispanic white.[47] It is evident that the ELMs do not represent the lay leadership grassroot developments in minority communities throughout the Catholic Church in the United States. We believe that any serious reflection on the nature and role of the ELM in the U.S. Church will have to take into consideration these grassroot developments.

For almost thirty years, I have been serving in South Florida as a Catholic school teacher, a parish director of religious education, a liturgical minister, a lay ministry formation and training agent at the archdiocesan level, and, most recently, as an academic dean at our college seminary. The ministerial experience has taken place primarily among Euro-Americans, Hispanic groups encompassing twenty-one Latin American and Caribbean countries, Haitians, Black Islanders, and some Filipino communities. The involvement with the African American community in the area has been very limited.

Some of the multicultural trends outlined above have already become evident in my own pastoral experience. According to the survey conducted in 1986 in preparation for the First Synod,[48] the Archdiocese of Miami is 63 percent Hispanic. The next three ethnic groups according to size are the "U.S. born White persons, the Haitians and the U.S. born Black persons." There is also an Asian-Pacific Islander presence in the archdiocese. This latter presence has become recently more evident.

From my involvement with the Filipino communities, I have learned of their extraordinary sense of Church and leadership abilities. The fact that the majority of their members are highly educated professionals such as doctors and nurses points toward a possible development of professional ELM among them. Nevertheless, this development may be delayed because they still do not have a public face in the larger community and are only beginning to claim their corporate identity as Filipino Catholics.

The Haitian community is the third largest ethnic group in the archdiocese. Some of them are the newest immigrants to South Florida. They have graced us with a deep-felt faith in the Lord, a gentle spirit, a strong sense of family and community, a remarkable love and reverence for the word of God, and a willingness to work. They are young, and they place high value on education: 95 percent of those under eighteen are enrolled in school.[49] But in spite of this giftedness, they are not able yet to function efficiently in the mainline Church. They have been confronted with unreasonable immigration regulations as well as with prejudice and discrimination from within the community—from the White, because of the color of their skin, and from the African American, because they do not share the same views and do not see themselves as Blacks, but as Haitians. They are a proud people with a strong sense of history. Nevertheless, the parishes that are mainly populated by Haitians show a tremendous and contagious enthusiasm for God and for the community.

The Hispanic community, which comprises 63 percent of the total archdiocesan population and 82 percent of Dade County (the most populated of the three counties), is the largest ethnic and cultural group in the archdiocese. Nevertheless, this community still does not have enough leadership roles in the parish at large, with the exception of those parishes that are highly populated by Hispanics and whose pastor is also Hispanic. We have been involved in parishes that although they were 60 percent Hispanic, had only one or two Hispanic representatives in the pastoral council.

Hispanics of any cultural background bring with them their enthusiasm and their eagerness to serve and to give some sort of communal expression to their faith. When leadership roles are not available in the parish at large, they frequently form small communities of prayer and Bible study groups. At times, these groups are parallel to the life of the mainline parish community.

In my experience in South Florida, I have found a large gap between a minority of highly educated Hispanics who are serving in the parish as DREs; in the archdiocesan level as directors and staff of departments; or in the Catholic institutions as professors and administrators; and the poorly educated Hispanics who are the natural leaders of their communities and who are affirmed by them. These persons are serving in detention centers, in evangelization, and in pastoral care ministries and are affirmed, admired, and looked up to by the members of their communities. These Hispanics are the natural leaders of their communities but, for the most part, would never appear as subjects in studies such as the ones reported in Zeni Fox's paper.

The members of all those ethnic and cultural groups who have graduated from the Ecclesial Lay Ministry Program of the Archdiocese of Miami report the need for role clarification, especially in their relationship with the employed parish ministers; they exercise leadership roles in all the broad areas of ministry presented above except, for the most part, in the area of organizational ministries; they definitely influence the formation of Christian community; they have been engaged in a thorough process of discernment of their call to ministry in which their communities and their leaders have been involved; and they have been officially commissioned by the archbishop to serve for a fixed period of time.

In summary, the research shows that the baptized are exercising a variety of leadership roles found under the educational, pastoral, and liturgical ministries of the Church. They perform them as remunerated and non-remunerated ministers. Although their contributions to the enhancement of parish life are highly accepted by pastors, clergy, and lay people,[50] the ELMs themselves feel the need for more affirmation and support. In addition, the research shows that the respondents are not fully representative of the diverse ethnic and cultural groups within the U.S. Catholic communities. The ecclesial lay ministers have a strong sense of vocation and do not see themselves as employed because of a shortage of priests.[51] There is a high level of satisfaction among the lay ministers; more than 40 percent see their work as a permanent commitment and would like to be officially installed in their roles.

It is apparent that the ELM event in the Church in the United States is a vibrant experience that presents some basic theological questions to the Christian community and its leadership as they approach the third millennium.

Theological Reflection

In this section, the present reality of the ELM will be evaluated in the light of the theological principles found in sections two and three of this paper. To do this, I will try to answer some of the theological questions that spring from the analysis of the reported data.

Leadership roles in the Church: baptism and its call, or orders? The theological principles found in the teaching of Vatican II and the surveyed literature seem to validate the experience of thousands of employed and volunteer lay and vowed religious men and women who are presently exercising formal leadership roles in the Church that were previously held by clergy. The council is explicit in its insistence that through the reception of the sacraments of baptism and confirmation *all are called to serve.*[52] From the fact of their union with Christ flows the lay person's right and duty to be an apostle, "it is by the Lord Himself that they are assigned to the apostolate . . ."[53] of building up the reign of God. In no. 5 of *Apostolicam Actuositatem*, we find that the laity, in the fulfillment of the

Church's mission, exercise their ministry (apostolate) both in the Church and in the world, "in both the spiritual and temporal orders."[54]

Nevertheless, it is significant that forms of a more official lay ministry as distinct from the general lay ministry are recognized by the council.[55] The council fathers state that the laity "have the capacity of being appointed by the hierarchy to certain ecclesiastical offices . . ."[56] In other words, participation in the general lay ministry does not require the approval of the ecclesiastical authority, but ecclesial lay ministry requires a special "mandate."[57]

It seems that the laity's justification for exercising leadership roles in the Church is based on the universal call to ministry received at baptism and on the receipt of a "mandate" from the hierarchy. The canonical paper prepared for this colloquium will aid in furthering the exploration of this issue.

What are some of the theological foundations for the processes of discernment and appointment? Although the different studies reported in Fox's paper did not show, for the most part, the existence of formal processes for the discernment of the call to ministry, elements of those processes were reported.[58] The following are some theological bases for the processes of discernment and appointment:

1. Ministry is irrevocably linked to the Christian community because of the central connection between the baptized and the welcoming community. Therefore, the call to ministry has to be discerned both by the minister and by the community that is the locus for ministries.

2. As a result of the baptismal state, it is from the union of the baptized with Christ himself that the call to ministry springs forth. Therefore, the sense of call and the willingness to serve ought to be important elements in a process of discernment.

3. There is a strong link between ministry and the Christian community's mission to build up the reign of God in both the spiritual and material realms. Consequently, the elements of giftedness, competence, and needs to be addressed play an important role in these processes.

4. If ecclesial ministry has to be authenticated by the hierarchy by some form of a mandate, the relationship with the ecclesial authority is another essential element in these processes.

Official rites of commissioning and installation: are they theologically justifiable? The link between ministry and the community and its mission, seems to justify the need for some sort of validation or recognition by the community for a ministry to be legitimate. This rite of commissioning or installation must be communal in nature; it is important for the baptized to have their gifts recognized by the community. The act of recognizing someone as a minister by the Church is decisive for the authentication of the call to share in the mission of the Church.

Although only 7 percent have presently a rite of commissioning, the ELM seems to view correctly the connection between the role of the community and some type of rite of installation.

Issues for Exploration

After reviewing the present reality of the ELM in light of the teachings on the nature of the sacrament of baptism and of the call to ministry, the following areas of questioning are proposed as issues in need of further exploration:

1. Since 21,800 men and women are currently enrolled in U.S. Catholic programs to prepare for lay ministry,[59] should the concept of ecclesial lay ministry include not only employed professional ministers but also volunteers who are graduates from lay ministry programs? If so, what are the differences between the *professional* and the *volunteer* and how do they relate to each other? Can *professionalism* create a new clericalism? What can the Church do about this?

2. In view that (a) ministry and the Christian community are irrevocably linked; (b) the process of discernment is basic to the call to ministry; (c) serving in a community to which one does not belong to is a contradiction; and (d) lay ministers engage in the process of discernment in the midst of the Christian community, what is the data on ELM saying to the *process of discernment* for the *call* to *ministry?*

3. The majority of the participants in the New Parish Ministers study are white (95%). What does this data say about a *multicultural Church* that will be overwhelmingly Hispanic by the year 2050?[60] What does it say to it?

Notes

1. National Conference of Catholic Bishops, *Called and Gifted for the Third Millennium* (Washington, D.C.: United States Catholic Conference, 1995), p. 15.

2. NCCB Subcommittee on Lay Ministry of the Committee on the Laity, "Description of the Focus of the Colloquium" (Washington, D.C.: July 22, 1996).

3. "Lumen Gentium," *Documents of Vatican II*, nos. 11, 12.

4. "Lumen Gentium," *Documents of Vatican II*, no. 10.

5. "Ad Gentes," *Documents of Vatican II*, no. 21.

6. *Rite of Christian Initiation of Adults*, General Introduction, 2 as cited by Julia Upton in "Baptism," *The New Dictionary of Theology*, Joseph A. Komonchak, Mary Collins, Dermont A. Lane, eds. (Wilmington, Del.: 1987), 79.

7. *Catechism of the Catholic Church*, Libreria Editrice Vaticana, nos. 1265-1270.

8. Ibid., no. 1268.

9. Ibid., no. 1267.

10. Ibid., no. 1265.

11. Ibid., no. 1269.

12. "Apostolicam Actuositatem," *Documents of Vatican II*, no. 3.

13. Ibid., no. 1270.

14. Ibid., no. 782

15. "Lumen Gentium," *Documents of Vatican II*, no. 11.

16. Ibid., no. 12.

17. Ibid.

18. "Apostolicam Actuositatem," *Documents of Vatican II*, no.3.

19. "Lumen Gentium," and "Apostolicam Actuositatem."

20. Yves M. Congar, OP, "My Path-Findings in the Theology of Laity and Ministries," *The Jurist* (Winter 1972): 178.

21. David N. Power, *Gifts that Differ: Lay Ministries Established and Unestablished* (New York: Pueblo Publishing Co., 1985), p. 61.

22. Edward Schillebeeckx, *Ministry: Leadership in the Community of Jesus Christ* (New York: Crossroad, 1981), p. 3.

23. Congar, *"My Path-Findings,"* pp. 182-183, 188; Power, *The Christian Priest: Elder and Prophet* (London: Sheed and Ward, 1973), pp. 12-13, 24; Power, *Gifts that Differ,* pp. 145, 186; Schillebeeckx, Ministry, p. 139.

24. Power, *Gifts that Differ,* p. 145.

25. Congar, *"My Path-Findings,"* p. 179.

26. Power, *Gifts that Differ,* p. 127.

27. Edward Schillebeeckx, *Ministry: Leadership in the Community of Jesus Christ* (New York: Crossroad, 1981), p. 45.

28. Power, *Gifts that Differ,* p. 145.

29. Thomas P. Rausch, *Catholicism at the Dawn of the Third Millennium* (Collegeville, Minn.: The Liturgical Press, 1996), p. 218. "In the nineteen thousand Catholic parishes in the United States about twenty thousand lay men and women are employed half-time or more in ministerial positions;" See James Heft paper, 3.

30. Fox, 4.

31. Ibid., 13.

32. Ibid., 2–5.

33. As cited by Zoila Diaz, *Critique of the Ecclesial Lay Ministry Program of the Archdiocese of Miami,* unpublished D.Min. dissertation (Washington, D.C.: The Catholic University of America, 1989), p. 30.

34. See Heft, 12, on the 1994 African Synod; Catholic Church documents describe wide and narrow views on evangelization. The wide view is reflected in *Evangelii Nuntiandi*: ". . . the task of evangelizing all people constitutes *the essential mission of the Church*," (EN, no. 14).

35. Fox, 4.

36. Ibid., 13, 5.

37. Ibid., 5.

38. Ibid., 10–11.

39. Ibid., 9–13.

40. Heft, 10–11; Fox, 20.

41. Fox, 19.

42. Ronaldo M. Cruz, *"The Hispanic Presence in the Catholic Church in the United States of America,"* unpublished report for the Inter-American Meeting of Bishops in Rio de Janeiro, Brazil (Washington, D.C.: USCC Secretariat for Hispanic Affairs, 1995), p. 2.

43. *Population Projections of the United States, by Age, Sex, Race, and Hispanic Origin: 1992 to 2050* (Washington, D.C.: United States Bureau of the Census), pp. 25–1092.

44. Ibid.

45. Cruz, 2.

46. Ibid., 4.

47. Fox, 7–8.

48. *Walking Together: First Synod 1985-1988* (Miami, FL.: Archdiocese of Miami, 1988), 13-16.

49. Ibid., 15.

50. Ibid., 12.

51. Ibid., 20.

52. "Apostolicam Actuositatem," *Documents of Vatican II*, no. 3.

53. Ibid.

54. Ibid., no. 5

55. "Lumen Gentium," no. 33.

56. Ibid.

57. "Apostolican Actuositatem," no. 24.

58. Fox, 9.

59. "Lay Ministers in Training—Who are They?" *Lay Ministry Update* (Washington, D.C.: NCCB Subcommittee on Lay Ministry, Jan/Feb., 1996), vol. 1, no. 1, 2.

60. *Population Projections*, p. 177.

Ministry in the Catholic Church Today: The Gift of Some Historical Trajectories

BY THOMAS O'MEARA, OP, PH.D.

What is in the history of the Church that speaks to ecclesial lay ministry? What are the precedents that shed light on the present situation? The following pages select a number of dynamic moments from the past that are influential in the Church today. Originally, they were times that brought forms and theologies to church life—forms and theologies born of the intersections between faith and culture. Those forms of ecclesiology or theology were important in the past, and they are still active today. They lie behind the emergence over the past three decades of parish and diocesan ministries beyond the priesthood and episcopacy. But their trajectories have differing modes of influence (reappearing, evolving, declining, dying). History is more than a library of precedents; it is a parent of what exists now, of what exists no longer, and of what is beginning to exist for the future. Five trajectories of Christian motifs and forms explain the recent expansion of ministry in the Catholic Church. They are

1. the Pauline theology of the Body of Christ with varied activities;

2. the social distinction between clergy and laity;

3. the ministry of women;

4. passing beyond the recent past; and

5. the reemergence of circles of ministry.

Ways of Seeing History

According to Christian faith, God does not disdain the historical condition of people on earth but does reveal his plan and destiny for people in history. God acts (through what we call *revelation* and *grace*) in a saving history. The special presence of the Trinity becomes concrete on earth in men and women within history, but, as its climax and paradigm Jesus of Nazareth, the risen Christ, shows the history of grace is not the same as secular history, although it speaks and acts in times and cultures.

In every age, there are people for whom history does not exist. They are not interested in the past and imagine all of human time to be much the same. They reject the idea of the temporal succession of human culture, or they presume that their adulthood or childhood embodies the perennial form of human life. Revealed religion can accidentally further this attitude: it can exalt a golden age (Moses at Sinai, the time of Jesus, the Middle Ages, Nüremberg at the time of Luther) holding a divine guarantee that no other age—all others are blank or corrupted by sin—can approach. However, Judaism leading to Jesus has a complex history, and the history of the Church over two millennia in its forms and articulations has considerable diversity. Fundamentalists and sects can fear time as a destroyer of tradition or as a goddess of novelty, but in fact the historical realizations of the Church in Edessa in the fifth century or in Naples in the sixteenth century are ways of continuing the Incarnation. Thomas Aquinas observed that in pondering something profound, time is our co-worker,[1] and the Gospel according to John concludes that it takes many human endeavors and languages to express all that was in Jesus (see John 21:25). Curiously, the Catholic restorationist, who identifies the Gospel with certain clothes from the 1880s, with one biblical translation, or with a vessel from the fifth or the fifteenth century has somewhat the same mind-set as the extreme feminist who rejects the past three millennia of cultures because their attitude toward women in public life was limited. Both fixate on one time—whether it is the past or today—and reject variety and progress. The deepest enemy of every fundamentalism is history.

A different approach to history, exemplified in the history of liturgies and spiritualities, expects both perdurance and alteration. To know a little about history, to understand a little of the Church's forms, whether in the catacomb chamber of the popes martyred under Decius in the third century or in the large structure of San Andrea della Valle, is to see that there are different ways in which the events and doctrines of Christianity (not expressed in exactly the same way in Jesus or Paul) have assumed useful and compelling forms in order to spread their message. While the Christian community must reject unfaithful and aberrant forms, it sees in its own history a variety of periods. For liturgies, religious orders, church offices, theologies, and devotions, a cultural time is a kind of lighting process. In one particular age, humanity understands itself in a particular way, and the Church uses the forms of human culture to give this or that perspective to life and faith. In no single time—not even in the decades immediately after Pentecost—can human beings express all there is in Christian realities. The Church, because of its evangelical nature, seeks out suitable forms for its worship and ministries, and history shows that the Spirit can inspire it to be present to diverse civilizations. This process is simply the continuing of the incarnation and builds upon a faith in the presence of the Spirit in the Church, so characteristic of the Catholic mind.[2]

There are two ways to view history. It has been commonplace to observe that Vatican II permitted the Church to reenter the flow of history without condemning it or being swept away by it. "I believe that the novelty of Vatican II," Yves Congar wrote, "consisted largely in its acceptance of the historicity of the Church, of Scripture, etc. . . . . The vision of the council has been resolutely that of the history of salvation completed by eschatology. . . . It is certain, or at least quite probable, that Vatican II will condition the life of the Church for a long time. That council incorporated a great density of faithfulness and wisdom coming from the entire Church; it is an event of a Pentecostal type."[3] Marked changes such as expansion in ministry have occurred recently around the world because the council prompted a look at today's ministerial needs and a look at the variety of ecclesiologies in biblical and patristic times—two perspectives made impossible by the perennial neoscholastic metaphysics dominant from 1860 to 1960. This permission for history to emerge is important for understanding the postconciliar period, precisely because history and culture drew forth so rapidly after 1965 forms and ideas—issues and problems that were only implicit in the documents, deliberations, and actions of the council.

The following pages sketch five trajectories, five "histories," five dynamic movements from Christian periods. They show past motifs and realizations of the Church at work, but they are active today. Each helps us understand the expansion of ministry taking place in the past twenty-five years.[4]

Trajectories of Church and Ministry

As previously identified, there are five trajectories of Christian motifs and forms that explain the recent expansion of ministry in the Catholic Church.[5] They are

1. the Pauline theology of the Body of Christ with varied activities;
2. the social distinction between clergy and laity;
3. the ministry of women;
4. passing beyond the recent past; and
5. the reemergence of circles of ministry.

Within the Body of Christ. A sign of living as a Christian is to find at times in one's life charisms becoming ministry. In recent centuries, we had a paucity of permanent charisms in the Church and only one full-time ministry named *priesthood.* Now, more and more Christians work in direct church ministry. There are many parishioners, young and old, who wish to work not simply in planning a picnic but in educating converts or bringing communion to the sick. Most pastors are assisted by several full-time ministries and by many part-time ones. Paul welcomed all ecclesial gifts, refusing to be embarrassed by or hostile to whatever was useful to the ministry of the Church. He minimized sensational gifts and accented those that were public services to the Gospel (in my view, charisms lead into the life of the Church and are the foundation for the ministries building up the community [cf. 1 Cor 12:7; 3:7,16; Rom 12:4]). Charism is the contact between the life of the Spirit and an individual personality. There can be many charisms ranging from momentary inspirations to lifelong decisions; at times in a Christian's life, we suspect, invitations will be given to serve the Church. Paul gave harmony to the diversity of important ministries, to communal services, by the metaphor of the human body with its many activities: "a unity in the work of service (διακονια), building up the body of Christ" (Eph 4:13). The "Body of Christ" presents a sociology of cooperation among ministries and actions in the Church. In the Christian community, a living organism, there is no inactive group and no spiritual elite. The ministering community precisely as active lives from the risen Christ, and does not merely revere his memory or memorize his words. Early Christian communities would not have understood a limiting of charism or ministry to a few.

Paul was faced with an explosion of charisms, and he hoped for a panoply of ministries. Paul's ecclesiology preserves universality, diversity, unity, power, and a lack of rivalry in a ministering community. Clearly, the lists of diaconal charisms in Romans, Corinthians, and Ephesians are not intended to exhaust or to control ministry. The ministry of leadership is mentioned by several names in the New Testament and is inevitably present in a community; leadership, however, is not the only ministry nor are other ministries derived from it (see 1 Cor 16:15).

The wider presence of New Testament ideas and the basing of ecclesiology upon biblical studies has influenced the expansion of ministry. In an unsettling way the dynamic parish of 1995 resembles a Pauline community in A.D. 55 perhaps more than it resembles a parish in 1945.[6]

Beyond the Distinction of Clergy and Laity. For a long time, the terms *clergy* and *laity*, based on the presence or absence of the rites of ordination (or tonsure), have divided the Church in two. The etymology of *clergy* lies in the Greek (κλεροσ), "lot," "portion." In Acts (1:15f) Matthias is elected by casting lots (κλερονσ) to receive the share (κλερον) of the apostolic ministry that Judas had abandoned. By the time of the *Apostolic Tradition* of Hippolytus (c. A.D. 220) the word was used for an ecclesiastical state (not a ministry) to which bishop, presbyters, and deacons (in Eastern churches, deaconesses?) belong. There is another New Testament meaning for κλεροσ. In Acts, Colossians, and Ephesians, the word is used for the share that all Christians—all members of a church—have in the word and reality of Christ, "the inheritance of the saints in light" (Col 1:12). Here κλεροσ means the share in eschatological salvation that God gives to each individual believer in the communion of all believers. This share is to be understood not simply as a fortunate "lot" but as a "good thing" prepared for the believer by God. A sharing in the Lord comes precisely not just to the clergy (the later κλερικοι) but to the whole People of God. And that breadth of the Spirit is the originality of Christianity (see Rom 8:1ff.).

During the third century, the focus of the community began to shift from evangelization to solemn liturgy and orthodox teaching, although the external mission of the Church was considerable. The separation of clergy from the people may have been nourished by the tendency of the churches to want to resemble the Jewish people of the inspired Pentateuch and to have similarities with their pagan neighbors' cults. Origen used κλερικοι as a term for those in special orders, and he contrasts them with all other Christians; he presented the clergy as the maintainers of the Church's organization, but with his enthusiasm for preaching and theology, he occasionally implied that the most important ministry is accomplished by those, at times not ordained, who teach and preach at an advanced level.

Class distinctions come in pairs. While the clergy became an elevated, sacral state, the laity became a passive group. The first Christians saw themselves as the People of God; a people open to all—male and female, slave and free, Jew and Greek (see Gal 3:28f). The idea of God's people with access to the Spirit through Jesus (often found in the New Testament writings) challenged the sacral religion of temples and cultic mysteries, and Hebrews, Ephesians, and 1 Peter mention the new covenant giving to all the followers of Christ a priestliness or consecration.

Λαικοσ, from which comes the Latin *laicus* and the English *laity,* has generally been thought to be simply an adjectival form of Λαοσ; in Christianity, a "lay person" was a member of the people who participated in the new covenant. Critical studies, however, have argued that this was not the case. In secular literature and in translations of the Old Testament after the Septuagint, the meaning of the word is much like our contemporary meaning: ordinary, outside, not holy, even profane. The word is rarely used in Christian literature before A.D. 200, but by the third century, Clement of Alexandria used the term of Christians who are not presbyters or deacons. (Slightly earlier, Tertullian, recalling previous theology, exclaimed: *"Nonne et laici sacerdotes sumus?"* "Are not we laity priests?") *Laity* became a term for the mass of Christians who are not among the ordained deacons, presbyters, and bishops. If the etymology and theology of Λαοσ, *people,* are positive, that of *laity* seems from its origins to have overtones of secular, passive, removed. Yves Congar has written: "To look for a 'spirituality of lay people' in the Scriptures makes no sense. There is no mention of laity. Certainly the word exists, but it exists outside the Christian vocabulary."[7] In American usage "lay person" means someone who is ignorant of the area under discussion, who is out of the field of action. Most meanings of the word are not positive, and ecclesial usage cannot escape their overtones.

As baptized Christians in large numbers undertake ministry in religious education, healthcare, or leadership and preaching in communities where no ordained ministers are available, neither biblical theology nor contemporary English meaning supports that word, which can denominate the baptized as *laity* in an extrinsic, passive sense. The fullness of baptism, the universal access to God, the avoidance of dualism, the basic equality of men and women in the kingdom of God—these biblical themes superseded subsequent divisions. One cannot make sense of today's parish in light of the clergy/laity distinction interpreted in a strict dualism.

In 1953, Congar had written the first theology of the laity, and he began: "It is not just a matter of adding a paragraph or a chapter to an ecclesiological exposition which from beginning to end ignores the principles on which a 'laicology' really depends. Without these [new] principles we should have, confronting a laicised world, only a clerical Church which would not be the People of God in the fullness of its truth. At bottom there can be only one sound and sufficient theology of laity, and that is a 'total ecclesiology'"[8] Twenty years later, after the council, reexamining his previous work, Congar concluded: "I have not written that ecclesiology."[9] His essay of 1972 intended to correct a vision "which at first was principally and unthinkingly clerical. . . . The Church of God is not built up solely by the actions of the official presbyterial ministry but by a multitude of diverse modes of service, stable or occasional, spontaneous or recognized, and, when the occasion arises consecrated, while falling short of sacramental ordination. These modes of service do exist . . . mothers at home, the person who coordinates liturgical celebrations or reads the sacred text, the woman visiting the sick or prisoners, adult catechists . . . . They exist now, but up to now were not called by their true name, *ministries*, nor were their place and status in ecclesiology recognized."[10]

A new—that is, an older—model was needed. "It is worth noticing that the decisive coupling is not 'priesthood/laity,' as I used it in *Jalons* [*Lay People in the Church*], but rather 'ministries/modes of community service.'"[11] Congar sketched a model that would replace the bipolar division of clergy and laity: a circle with Christ and Spirit as ground or power animating ministries in community. He continued: "It is necessary to substitute for the linear scheme a scheme where the community appears as the enveloping reality *within* which the ministries, eventually the instituted sacramental ministries, are placed as *modes of service* of what the community is called to be and do."[12]

The venerable model of clergy and laity is incapable of interpreting realistically what the Church has already become in many parts of the world. When the magisterium defends that distinction, it is defending not the words, not a dualism, and not a division in the Church between those solely active and those largely passive; it is legitimately defending the distinction between ministries. That the ministry of pastor is central and more important than that of reader is obvious, but the ministry of reader is not nothing, not a tolerated usurpation of clerical activity. Ministries differ in importance and distinctions among ministries (and ministers) remain, but they are, according to the New Testament, grounded upon a common faith and baptismal commissioning.

Women in Ministry. There is a trajectory for the ministries of women. It reaches from the New Testament to the present day, but it also passes through centuries of neglect and minimalization. The ministry of women, however, does not appear in modern times in the form of the *apostles* or *deaconesses* of the first centuries but in the activities of women religious. The growing presence of women in ministry today has followed, after 1970, upon the work of women religious, and their history that began in the twelfth century. There were precursors to Francis's and Dominic's ideal of traveling evangelical groups, and these included women who desired to imitate Jesus' life and preaching. It seems that Dominic wanted to draw women into the activities of countering the Albigensians, but the Church led the female counterparts to the friars back into cloistered life. There they remained.[13] In the seventeenth century, by combining cloistered forms with some active ministry, women religious were permitted to work in education and health care, and after a century or more, this led to active religious congregations (often begun as assemblies of celibate women in a private association for some work).

The United States with a thousand and more schools, hospitals, and other institutions has been the modern display ground of the congregations of active women religious. Women religious did not hesitate to establish in the most difficult circumstances all kinds of institutions, most of whose works correspond to Pauline ministries. If we consider health care, religious education, the care of the poor, and retreat houses to be ministries, then one must conclude that more than 60 or 70 percent of Catholic ministry in the United States during the twentieth century has been done by women. The time of these large, expanding, ministering congregations is coming to an end, but this trajectory leads to something beyond.

If, before Vatican II, women in the Catholic Church entered ministry through religious congregations, in the first decade of the post-conciliar era, many sisters entered new and more directly ecclesial ministries; and by the early 1970s, women not belonging to religious congregations are prominent in ministry. Motifs from the council such as the charismatic, ministerial, and priestly aspects of baptism; the welcome by parishes of Catholics who are not religious into ministries; a more subtle understanding of the presences of grace; the opening of the church's ministry beyond the Sunday Masses; and the dignity of having been drawn into the kingdom of God—these have led to a further stage of women in ministry.

Passing beyond the Recent Past. The Baroque, reaching from 1580 to 1720, was an epochal period. That time of cultural renewal and of religious expansion was, more than the Tridentine Counter-Reformation, the Catholic restoration and renewal called the Baroque; it is the most recent major era in Roman Catholic life. With variations, it reappeared and continued from 1820 to 1960. With Vatican I, world-wide Catholicism began to leave the Baroque.

The Baroque spirit brought to the Church new theologies, spiritualities, and arts, and these usually manifested interplays between personality and grace (e.g., as articulated by Ignatius Loyola, Philip Neri, or Teresa of Avila). A universality begun by Columbus' exploration and Galileo's astronomy offered to the Catholic mind a new world view. God was experienced in a vastness, freedom, and goodness flowing through a world of diversity, movement, and order, while Christ appeared in a more human way, filled with a personal love—redemptive and empowering. This was a time of great missionary work and great interior conversations with the divine. Actual grace, the central theme of the Baroque, moved from God to people, a transient force influencing adolescent vocations, validly received sacraments, or death-bed decisions; grace was a power for life, a force to aid each individual in following God's will, a force contacting the will and emotions more than the intellect. The Baroque furthered systems: for example, methods of prayer and meditation. Sixtus V gave an early example of modern urban planning for the streets and basilicas of Rome, and Bernini's ensemble of St. Peter's church and piazza mirrored centralized papal authority. Since the Baroque world is also a theater (buildings, city squares, churches, palaces, halls, and baldachinos set off human performance), Baroque Christianity was filled with the visions and ecstasies of martyrs, missionaries, and stigmatics. Ornate statues told emotional stories, and crowds passively attended liturgies like folk missions, novenas to saints, or rites surrounding the blessed sacrament. The Baroque went underground during the Enlightenment and then reemerged, albeit with some new emphases, as Romanticism moved beyond the Enlightenment. The nineteenth century had its originality (it added a neomedieval restoration), but that age more often than not composed variations on the Baroque. That time from 1830 to 1960 is the period just before Vatican II, and it has its theology of priestly, consecrated, and ministerial life and activity.

What were the characteristics of ministry from the Baroque to Vatican II? Ministry was done by parish priests limited largely to sacraments and by members of religious orders who conducted a number and variety of ministries from running a university in Lima to an orphanage in New York City. It was an activist ministry strengthened by a theology of actual graces brought by sacraments and by personal prayer. Other baptized

Christians might help in the physical support of running a hospital or preaching the Gospel in a foreign country, but they were kept at a distance from the real, public ministry, just as they were kept from the sanctuary. There were overtones that ministry was largely about the methods of spirituality and the rubrics of liturgy, that the fallen world could receive only so much redemption, and that all not under orders or vows remained in a secular sphere capable not of ministry but of a vague witness. The "Apostolate of the Laity" confirmed this, adding an incorrect ecclesiology that caritative functions alone were possible as services in the Church and that the works of the laity derived from minor shares in the episcopal office.[14]

The understanding of ministries flowing out of baptism and expanding around the leadership of pastor and bishop; a rejection of the strict separation of secular and sacred; grace no longer viewed within the context of a waterworks of laws and definitions; a view that there were ministries that existed outside of liturgy; the involvement of the baptized in liturgy itself; the joining of meditation with liturgy and public action—these drew the Baroque trajectory into something new.

As a bridge between the end of the Baroque and the developments after Vatican II of women and men in ministries, we note an important historical-sociological study. It is important because of the decline in the numbers of members of religious orders, which, along with the decline in the diocesan priesthood, presents a puzzling, uncomfortable situation, but perhaps one indicating a new direction. Raymond Hostie, a Belgian sociologist, searched the histories of *all* religious orders in the Western Church and found in them a similar life cycle. He delineated stages of foundation, solidification of identity, flourishing, decline, and demise. The cycle lasts about 130 years. All orders have gone and go through this cycle—but most go through it only once. The Benedictines, the Franciscans, and the Jesuits have gone through it several times.[15] Today, we see the demise of some religious orders of men and of many religious orders of women. In light of Hostie's study, this is not surprising— we find ourselves at the end of a cycle begun when many, many religious orders came into existence after the French Revolution and during the romantic restoration after 1830. The many congregations of women religious in this century in America are largely the gift of this recent period; this ministerial time has brought their great ministerial accomplishments, but its characteristic of great numbers is ending.

We might conclude that ahead will be new religious orders—and that might be. Will there be a fourth form of religious life ranking with monks, friars, and active orders (the unimaginative imitation of religious life in the 1940s, which has produced a few groups since 1980, is not significant)? It is possible, however, that such a future is not the plan of the Holy Spirit. It may be that for the numbers and need of ministries, even tens of thousands of vowed men and women are not adequate (although they remain important). More ministers are needed to work among the great number of believers and nonbelievers: for ministering to their graced lives with some individuality, for meeting heightened levels of education in the Untied States and cultural diversity in the world, and for engaging the great works of mercy and evangelization that a large global population needs. The end of this recent cycle of religious life is indeed leading ahead. But it may be leading into broader modes and kinds of ministry; in short, into a Church of ministers, many with the same education as priests and religious. These are the people who have entered education and ministry in the past three decades.

The Reappearance of Baptismal Ministry. Trajectories three and four lead us to today's Church in the United States. In the years after 1965, the ministry changed rapidly. As soon as the council had ended, suddenly Catholic men and women began in great numbers to study theology and to study for the ministry (there were only one or two places in 1960 where a noncleric could study theology; by 1975, it took the *National Catholic Reporter* several issues to list them). This remarkable phenomenon had its own preparation. Various organizations were founded in the century or so after 1830, which drew individual Christians into active groups; these ranged from third orders and confraternities to Catholic Action, the Vincent de Paul and Holy Name Societies, Jocists, and urban houses of Christian witness. But they were qualitatively different from today's expansion of ministry, for they—taking for granted the distinction of sacral and sacred worlds—did not pass beyond witness and material assistance into the essential ministries of the Church. In the 1970s, parishioners' activities underwent a pneumatic metamorphosis as men and women (and permanent deacons) became active in liturgical ministries during and outside of Mass as well as in services of education, liturgy, peace and justice, music, and ministry to the sick and dying. If we focus on the basic place of ministry—the parish, from 1965 to 1975—parishes changed in terms of which ministries were done and in terms of who did them. The parish was no longer a place of rapid Masses and group baptisms in Latin with an occasional picnic or parish dance. The liturgy, including deacons, lectors, cantors, and communion bearers, illustrates the expansion of the ministry outside of Sunday morning in church. Change in the ministerial pattern of parish and diocesan life did not come from bishops, nor from the methodologies of theologians, nor from sociological surveys of the Catholic Church, nor from academic observers of religion in the United States. The expansion of ministry did not come from the decline in the number of priests: the ministries of baptized men and women were often ministries that had not existed for some centuries. Moreover, sociological surveys have shown that the decline in numbers of priests and religious, although it was not to become evident until the late 1960s, had begun before the council and was probably tied to changes in the aspirations of Catholics who were no longer of an immigrant world. In North America, and in succeeding years in other parts of the world, the very model of parish ministry changed.[16] A dialectic is at work—the ministry expands because there is more to do, and such an expansion of ministries is possible because people are seeking ministry.

Conclusion

The trajectories just sketched are realizations of ministry in the past and explanations of ministry in the present and the future. They were stimulated by a culture and an age; they are at work, diversely, in the Catholic Church today. Each trajectory brings us to our present situation and suggests that this new situation is neither utterly new nor unexpected. The theology of the Body of Christ indicates that ministry for the baptized should be ordinary; history indicates that the ministries of women have existed; the present age has brought a model that goes beyond the sole performance of whatever was being done by clergy or by religious and priests.

Change is neither an instantaneous revolution nor a chain of successes. In old and huge organizations like the Catholic Church, change is a complex phenomenon. The past never fully disappears; old forms are not fully replaced; the new must be both incarnational and traditional. If these shifts in church life are considerable and fraught with further implications, nonetheless, their day-to-day realization in the life of the local church is ordinary.

Why did this change come about? It seems unavoidable to conclude that it came from a deep encounter between the Spirit of the risen Jesus and the People of God. Apparently, the Holy Spirit intends to alter, to broaden the way in which the Church's members understand themselves and the Church's mission. Perhaps the Spirit wants to restore the primal Christian reality of wider ministry and to end the centuries in which most Christians were viewed as passive or even second-class citizens in the Church.

What these pages have described, a leaving and a beginning, is a difficult passage, but it is the unavoidable present time, a time that Pope Paul VI, opening the second session of Vatican II, said had come to free "the noble and destiny-filled name of 'church'" from "forms full of holes and close to collapse."[17] To reflect upon the expansion of ecclesial ministry in the past few decades is to conclude that the Spirit is determined to bestow on more people more ministries, and to disclose to the world Church how much there remains to be done.

Notes

1. Thomas Aquinas, "Time is, so to say, a discoverer and a kind of co-operator." *Commentary on the Ethics of Aristotle*, 2, 4.

2. "Consequently the mystery of Christ's Incarnation was to be believed in all ages and by all peoples in some fashion—but in diverse ways according to the differences of times and peoples." Thomas Aquinas, *Summa theologiae*, II–II, 2, 7.

3. Congar, "Situation écclésiologique au moment de 'Ecclesiam suam' et passage à une église dans l'itinéraire des hommes," *Le Concile de Vatican II* (Paris: Beauchesne, 1984), 27; *Fifty Years of Catholic Theology: Conversations with Yves Congar*, B. Lauret, ed. (Philadelphia: Fortress, 1988), 8; "Regard sur le Concile Vatican II (à l'occasion du 20e anniversaire)," *Le Concile Vatican II*, 68. Congar did not think that the upheavals in the post-conciliar era had their roots in Vatican II but, rather, in the constrictive decades or centuries before it. "The years after the council are a global phenomenon with world-wide dimensions. A crisis would have come anyway. The council assisted its entry into the Church by ending the isolation of the Church, by giving a wider audience to the Church, and by ending a monolithic institution protected by fictions. The present time is linked to the gigantic change which touches culture, the ways of life in society and the 'cohumanity' around the world." *Une passion. L'unité* (Paris: Cerf, 1974), 109. "I do not believe that the present crisis in the Church is the result of Vatican II . . . the realities that preoccupy us today were already present or beginning to appear in the 1950s and even in the 1930s." Congar, "A Last Look at the Church," in A. Stacpoole, *Vatican II Revisited* (Minneapolis: Winston, 1986), 351. "It is astonishing how the post-conciliar period has so little to do with the council. . . .The post-conciliar questions are new and radical, and *aggiornamento* [now] means changes and adaptations to a new situation, assuming the principles of the original institution." Private letter of September 12, 1970. "All the work of the council is a half-way station." J. Puyo, *Une vie pour la vérité* (Paris: Centurion, 1975), 149. It is interesting to ponder how the influx of large number of vocations into the pre-conciliar Church was to be a factor in the alteration of religious life and ministry, for they entered and furthered the post-conciliar Church.

4. In his essay on not just charisms in the Church but the charismatic reality of the Church, Karl Rahner argued for the presence and plan of the Spirit. "The Spirit and grace constitute the Church as an eschatological reality." ("Bemerkungen über das Charismatische in der Kirche," *Schriften zur Theologie IX* [Einsiedeln: Benziger, 1970], 416 [*Theological Investigations*, 10]). What is the charismatic? It is not a violent, anti-institutional sensational phenomena but the role of the Spirit viewed dynamically in history. For Rahner, "the charismatic in the Church" means the varied but universal presence of the Spirit at a level of depth that then prompts the personal and ecclesial realizations which make grace concrete or which reduce and deform the intention of the Spirit. This is "the first, the most proper and ecclesial among the formal essential characteristics of the Church" (431). Consequently, the Church is "not a closed but an open system, that is, the kind of community whose concrete condition as already given and as coming to be cannot fully be determined from a single point within itself, but from a point outside of itself, from God, so that each condition of the system can rightly be said to be effected charismatically and not institutionally" (423).

5. "Christian ministry is the public activity of a baptized follower of Jesus Christ flowing from the Spirit's charism and the individual personality on behalf of a Christian community to witness to, serve and realize the kingdom of God." O'Meara, *Theology of Ministry* (Mahwah, N.J.: Paulist, 1983), 142.

6. In the years just before the council, the U.S. parish was full of repressed vitality, but Sunday morning had little connection with the descriptions of church and ministry that were read at Mass in the letters of the New Testament. What did it mean to say that all Christians were to be active in the Body of Christ when they sat passively facing forward in church pews? What did Paul intend with ideas about a public liturgy of preaching and life and all kinds of services when the activities of the sole minister were silent and isolated? Why read a list of ministries in Paul's letters to the Romans and Corinthians when there was only one activity in a church, that of the priest? The word *ministry* was a Protestant term not used by Catholics, and *charism* was something that tried to make a dangerous figure like Catherine of Siena or Dorothy Day respectable. Clearly, in terms of the history of ministry and ministries, while the Gospel is present and presented in the Church at all times, its realization in ecclesial tradition in some ages can be diminished.

Pauline theology gave what became, with difficulty in theological expression and practical realization, the ecclesial traditional theology of the Church and its actions. Charism was a communal reality, and the community, Christians in other ministries, and the community leader had roles in discerning the presence of the Spirit. For Catholicism, verification of the presence of the Spirit includes signs of evangelical discipleship, perdurance and success in service over time, and personal holiness. How this is verified in the long history of the Church—examples of ecclesial and personal success and failure in discerning the Spirit—requires precise historical analysis.

7. Congar, "Laic et Laicat," *Dictionnaire de Spiritualité* 9 (Paris: Desclée, 1976), 79.

8. Congar, *Lay People in the Church. A Study for a Theology of Laity* (Westminster: Newman, 1957), xvi. Congar wrote: "The responsibility of witness and service flows from the Christian quality as such: thus there is mission in the broad sense, and this mission is equally incumbent on every Christian. All the disciples received the Holy Spirit and the gifts which render them responsible for God's cause." Congar, *Le Concile au jour le jour* [Session IV] (Paris: Cerf, 1966), 61. In the French milieu "lay" in the course of the nineteenth century and into this century took on the meaning of secular, anti-clerical forces intent upon legal means to reduce the influence of the Church; hence the word now can be employed only with constant theological reinterpretation.

9. Congar, *"My Path-Findings . . . ,"* 169.

10. Ibid., 181.

11. Ibid., 176.

12. Ibid., 178.

13. Teachers and advisers like Meister Eckhart and Johannes Tauler indicate a high level of education, preaching, and spiritual direction within women's monasteries, and Thomas Aquinas mentions women preaching in their own communities (*Summa theologiae*, II–II, 177, 2).

14. "Not a hierarchology," Congar, *Ministères et communion écclésiale* (Paris: Cerf, 1971), 10. Congar described the institutionalized ecclesiology, which had lasted almost four centuries. "We can note the ecclesiological aspect of Roman centralization, which is linked to a further important aspect. Trent had affirmed in the face of Protestantism that Christ is not solely a redeemer but that he is also a law-giver. In this line, even in its work at sustaining and demanding a kind of bishop who was truly pastoral, it favored the construction of a hierarchical order, but not one arranged around the Eucharist but around the 'regime' of which Rome occupies the center and summit. Despite the admirable expansion of Christian life and pastoral ministry, an era of legalism began, replacing a somewhat theoretical ecclesiology. Finally an orthodoxy, not only of faith but of theology, is fixed by a kind of canonization of the conceptual and verbal system come down from scholasticism which from then to our own times has incorporated itself into Catholicism." In *L'Église de saint Augustin à l'époque moderne* (Paris: Cerf, 1970), 368. The ecclesiology of the neoscholastic manuals can be found in a textbook by Gerard Paris, widely used in the studia of Dominican Order: the *Tractatus de ecclesia Christi ad mentem S. Thomae Aquinatis* (Malta: Muscat, 1949) presented the four causes of the Church in Aristotelian language: the formal cause was the bishops; the efficient cause was Jesus, the Holy Spirit, and the bishops; the final cause was heaven; the material cause, like clay for a statue, was everyone who was not a bishop, provincial, or pastor.

15. Hostie, *Vie et mort des ordres religieux. Approches psychsociologiques* (Paris: Desclée de Brouwer, 1972); for a summary, see R. Fitz and L. Cada, "The Recovery of Religious Life," *Review for Religious* 34 (1975): 690ff.

16. One often finds what seem to be new ideas in unlikely sources. Not long after 1500, Thomas de Vio, Cardinal Cajetan wrote: "The faithful, because they are moved by the Holy Spirit to the works of their spiritual life . . . , act as parts of one totality. . . . Each faithful believes they are members of the church, and as a member of the church believes, hopes, ministers the sacraments, receives, teaches, learns, etc, and on behalf of the church does these things as a part of the whole to whom they [the activities] all belong." *Commentaria Cardinalis Caietani* on *Summa theologiae* II–II, 39, 1 in Sancti Thomae Aquinatis, *Opera Omnia* , Leonis XIII, P. M., edita, vol. 8 (Rome: Typographia Polyglotta, 1895), 307.

17. Paul VI, "Allocutio Secunda SS. Concilii Periodo Ineunte," *Acta Apostolicae Sedis* (Sept. 29, 1963), *AAS* 55 (1963): 895.

Biblical Foundations for
Christian Ministry BY DIANNE BERGANT, CSA, PH.D.

After preliminary remarks about the revitalization of biblical theology and the limitations of searching for biblical foundations for pastoral practices, the paper surveys leadership roles in the Old Testament and briefly examines the New Testament's proclamation of Jesus as the fulfillment of messianic expectation. It looks at the judge, the king, the prophet, and the priest as individuals seized by the Spirit of the Lord and enabled to do things— always for the good of the entire community—that were beyond their ordinary abilities. "While all of these roles grew out of the needs of the people and enjoyed a certain religious legitimation, some became part of the religio-political structure of Israel and others did not." All of them point to the messianic age when the Spirit is given to all.

In the New Testament, the Gospels witness to the messianic character of the ministry of Jesus—a ministry that embodies the earlier roles. Other Christian writings in the New Testament highlight the characteristics of Christian ministry—the most fundamental being service—and "exhort the Christians to unity amidst this diversity of Spirit-filled manifestations." The paper concludes with the reminder that this is the time of the Spirit.

Preliminary Remarks

B efore addressing the topic assigned to me for this colloquium, it is important to make two points. First, one of the pivotal theological effects of Vatican II is the revitalization of biblical theology. While this turn to the Bible continues to manifest itself in many ways, one of the most significant has been the search to discover the biblical foundation or justification of current pastoral practice. This search has resulted in the retrieval of much rich theological, pastoral, and spiritual tradition. It has also provided the Church with an appreciation for the ongoing presence and direction of the Spirit of God and insight into the theological development that it has brought forth.

Second, it is important to be aware of the limitations of the methodological approach used in any search for the biblical foundation for pastoral practice. In some circles, what is called biblical theology is really a use of biblical passages as proof-texts to legitimate a theological conclusion or pastoral practice. This technique does not read the biblical material within its own literary or historical contexts and, consequently, does not accurately deal with the theological meanings that the text itself might yield. In more critical circles, the approach most often used today is some form of historical criticism. It can be very helpful in our search for any historical precedent. However, looking for precedents or biblical foundations is both enhancing and limiting. While history is an important factor in our tradition and precedents can ground our practices, the ongoing presence of the Spirit frequently brings forth realities that are new. Precedent can too often proscribe.

By means of critical historical research, we have been able to trace the biblical roots of some current practice. On the other hand, while faithful to the biblical tradition, other practice appears to be more a reinterpretation of the tradition and/or an innovative pastoral response to pressing needs. In the biblical material examined for this study, it is clear that the responsibility of ministry is a direct result of the anointing by the Spirit, and, in the Christian tradition, it is more a universal call than a particular one. In other words, one will have to look elsewhere for the specific roots of ecclesial lay ministry as defined for this colloquium.

Introduction

Central to our lives as Christians is the privilege and responsibility of being part of the saving action of God. This participation is deeply rooted within our biblical tradition. In tracing these biblical roots, this paper begins with a survey of certain leadership roles found in the Old Testament of the Bible. It will show that, while all of these roles grew out of the needs of the people and enjoyed certain religious legitimation, some became part of the religio-political structure of Israel and others did not. While this paper will focus on those roles that are considered charismatic or Spirit-filled, their relationship with other more institutionalized roles will be noted.

This survey of ancient Israelite leadership will be followed by a brief examination of the New Testament's proclamation of Jesus as the fulfillment of messianic expectation. It is within such a biblical context that Christian ministry can be perceived as the ongoing unfolding of the charismatic and messianic ministry of the Lord Jesus.

Charismatic Leaders of the Old Testament

Within the early traditions of biblical Israel, the Spirit of the Lord was understood as a principle of dynamic divine action, not as a separate divine manifestation as is found in later Christian thought (i.e., the third person of the Trinity). This divine Spirit was a force that had unique effects in human history. Those who received the Spirit, or more accurately those who were seized by the Spirit, were thus empowered to act within the community in some unique fashion. The particular needs of the community determined the character of this action. In other words, God's saving power was brought to the community through the agency of certain individuals.

In order to assure that the wondrous power was ascribed to God, the stories insist that these were not necessarily people who already possessed uncommon ability. On the contrary, the qualities necessary to accomplish the particular mission were conferred on the individual with the coming of the Spirit. In most cases, this gift or *charisma* was a temporary power. When the community emergency passed, or the pressing need had been met, the particular charismatic role was no longer required, and the power of the Spirit withdrew. Regardless of the length of time that one was under the influence of the Spirit or the transformative effects that this had on that individual's personal life, the Spirit was given for the good of the entire community and not merely for the sake of the charismatic person. The one possessing or possessed by the Spirit was the instrument through which the saving power of God was communicated to others.

The religious traditions of the biblical Israel, as found within its earliest writings, testify to the character of the people's historical consciousness. For them, history was the recounting of the experience of the saving God in the events of life. We do not find here accounts of women and men taken up into the mystical realms of the divine, as are found in some of the religious traditions of other ancient Near-Eastern cultures. Instead, the biblical narratives describe the God of Israel entering the lives of ordinary women and men. There on the stage of human history, the religious encounter between the divine and the human took place. The broad diversity of human experience and the conviction of the ever-present saving activity of God resulted in belief in a variety of divine manifestations.

The limitations of space prevent us from considering here every instance of charismatic or Spirit-filled leadership found in the Bible. This paper examines briefly the judge, the king, the prophet, the priest, and the mysterious figure of the messianic age.

The Judge

During the time of tribal confederacy (1200–1060 B.C.E.), the people were held together more by common religious confession than by political ties. The central shrine, whether Shechem, Shiloh, or Gilgal, symbolized Israel's tribal unity, and the central figure at the shrine city was frequently a judge of Israel. Although God clearly was held to be the head of this tribal confederacy, the judge was God's representative before the people. The primary responsibility of the judge was to preserve and to interpret divine law to which the people were subject (e.g., Deborah [Jgs 4–5]; Samuel [1 Sm 7:6]). Judges were not merely officials with authority to administer justice by trying cases in law. Many of them were tribal military heroes raised up by the Spirit of the Lord at given times of emergency to deliver the People of God from enemies who might destroy them. In a certain sense, the judges brought the vindication of divine justice to the battlefield:

The spirit of the LORD enveloped Gideon; he blew the horn that summoned Abiezer to follow him. (Jgs 6:34)

The spirit of the LORD came upon Jephthah . . . , (he) went on to the Ammonite to fight against them, and the LORD delivered them into his power. (Jgs 11:29, 32)

The spirit of the LORD came upon [Samson], and he went down to Ashkelon, where he killed thirty of their men and despoiled them. (Jgs 14:19)

These narratives state that the leaders were seized by some impulse of the Spirit, which led them to do or to say things that were beyond their ordinary abilities. In reality, their authority may well have been derived from personal, physical, or psychological attributes that set them apart from the commonplace. However, since it was personal, exclusive, and independent of any hierarchic structure, according to ancient Israel the source of these attributes was the "spirit of the Lord." Thus the judges were believed to be divine agents with ultimate authority.

Since the basis of this kind of charismatic authority was personal ability, the status of the judge was not hereditary as was the case in patriarchal-tribal system. It was dependent neither on social status (Jephthah was the son of a harlot [Jgs 11:1]), nor on age (Gideon was youngest in his family [Jgs 6:15], nor on sex (Deborah [Jgs 4–5]). Furthermore, the judges may have been associated with shrines, but their authority does not appear to have been derived from that association. Finally, their authority did not rely on coercion, for the armies that they were able to raise were composed of voluntary militia and not conscripts.

As effective as such charismatic leadership may have been, it failed in some very crucial areas. First, most of the judges dealt with local issues. No one of them was ever able to unite the entire confederacy around some common effort, although Deborah seems to have been more successful at this than most. Second, such leadership had to be reestablished at the death of each judge. Continual military and political insecurity prompted Israel to institutionalize the charism of leadership in the form of the monarchy. Such stabilization was considered a political necessity, and, though there was significant opposition to this move in the beginning (1 Sm 8), it eventually gained support and religious legitimation (1 Sm 9–10).

The King
At different periods in the history of ancient Israel, the dynamic power of God seems to have manifested itself through different groups of

people in different ways. It moved the judges to act in one way and the kings to act in another. The judges were military deliverers; the kings may have been warriors, but their primary responsibilities were as social and political administrators. Despite this difference, the source of leadership of both judge and king was ascribed to the Spirit of the Lord:

Then Samuel, with the horn of oil in hand, anointed him in the midst of his brothers; and from that day on, the spirit of the LORD rushed upon David. (1 Sm 16:13)

While the Spirit of the Lord came upon the judge only in times of crisis and remained for the duration of the specific critical period, the Spirit was thought to reside permanently with the king, unless taken away as punishment, as was the case with Saul (1 Sm 16:14). The conferral of the Spirit on the monarch was ritually symbolized by means of anointing. This anointing made the king a sacred person, set apart and deserving of respect. This explains David s unwillingness to inflict harm on Saul even though the king had set out to destroy him:

[David] said to his men, "The LORD forbid that I should do such a thing to my master [Saul], the LORD'S anointed, as to lay a hand on him, for he is the LORD'S anointed." (1 Sm 24:7, cf. 26:9–11)

The biblical story suggests that, initially, kingship was charismatic, bestowed on whomever God chose. It was during the time of David that the monarchy became an institution and hereditary succession—not an undisputed blessing—was introduced (cf. 2 Sm 7:11–17). Still, an element of charismatic royal leadership never really died, especially in the northern kingdom. The biblical story does not always include accounts of the spirit coming upon northern kings, thus conferring divine approval on their leadership. Most likely, this is because the stories are told from the point of view of the south, which clearly condemned the secession of the ten northern tribes. The closest we come to such a narrative is the report of Jeroboam's encounter with the prophet Ahijah (1 Kgs 11:30–31). However, even this story confers only general divine approval on the northern kingdom and this approval is not specific to its leadership.

It appears that in the initial stages of its political development, leadership in ancient Israel was generally charismatic. It was only later, when the structures of society became somewhat standardized that leadership itself was more specifically defined. The structural expression that this leadership took was usually borrowed from the society at large (e.g., ancient Near-Eastern forms of monarchic rule). These structures both developed and limited the charismatic possibilities. The religious history of Israel shows that whenever religion became identified too closely with the political system, it was challenged by another charismatic manifestation—prophetic critique.

The Prophet

The primary manifestation of the Spirit of the Lord in the traditions of biblical Israel is prophecy. Several prophets themselves speak of being overcome by the Spirit:

> *But as for me, I am filled with the power, with the spirit of the LORD . . . .* (Mi 3:8)

> *Then the spirit of the LORD fell upon me. . . .* (Ez 11:5)

Theories of prophetic possession are usually characterized by the belief that the Spirit takes control of individuals and speaks through them to the rest of the people, with the result that the speech of the prophet is really the speech of the Spirit. For this reason, prophecy is described as the reception and delivery of the word of God. This stress on God's word is more characteristic in prophetic literature than is reference to possession by the Spirit:

> *My spirit which is upon you and my words which I have put into your mouth. . . .* (Is 59:21)

> *The word of the LORD that came to Hosea. . . .* (Hos 1:1)

> *The word of the LORD came to me thus. . . .* (Jer 1:4)

Other accounts of the prophetic call report the visionary character of the divine–human communication:

> *The words of Amos, a shepherd from Tekoa, which he received in vision concerning Israel. . . .* (Am 1:1)

> *The vision which Isaiah, son of Amoz, had concerning Judah and Jerusalem. . . .* (Is 1:1)

> *The word of the* LORD *which came to Micah of Moresheth . . . the vision he received concerning Samaria and Jerusalem.* (Mi 1:1)

The basic purpose of prophecy was to impart revelation and to act as its authentic interpreter. Sent by God in order to impart God's thought, the prophets were compelled to repeat what they had heard (Jer 23:28). Their authority lay in the content of their message: it called the people to faith in the one and only God; it charged them to live this faith through devotion to God and love of neighbor; it offered them a vision, in broad outlines, of the messianic age to come.

A careful examination of prophecy in Israel shows a very intimate and tension-filled relationship between it and the monarchy. Some have even claimed that this charismatic force grew up within Israel as its religious conscience, calling the people and especially the leadership back to covenantal fidelity. The more the monarchy sought to protect itself rather than fulfill its covenantal responsibilities, the more the prophets challenged its behavior. Still, once established, the monarchy itself does not seem to have been rejected by the prophets. Instead, it was called to reform.

The Priest

Another group of religious leaders that played an important role in Israel's history was the priesthood. Priests appear in some of the exodus narratives (e.g., Ex 19:22) as well as those recounting the time of the judges (e.g., Eli at Shiloh in 1 Sm 1–3). However, the priestly tradition itself was a much later development, and so much of what we read in these early narratives is anachronistic. While the priests were indeed religious leaders, their primary function was cultic. Even when they provided "torah teaching," it was normally within a ritual context.

Rather than being personally called to religious leadership by God as were judges, early kings, and prophets, priests were either appointed or born into a priestly family. Like the monarchy after David, the priesthood was hereditary. The genealogies of the priestly families shows their need for religious legitimation (Ex 6:14–26). Other narratives show how dependent the priesthood was upon royal patronage (1 Sm 30:7). Individual priests may have been holy intermediaries, but the institution itself was not charismatic. Worship was integral to the lives of the people and, therefore, so were cultic leaders. However, because they were a part of the institution, their loyalties frequently were more political than religious.

The Messianic Age

Virtually all of the prophets shared some kind of vision of an idyllic future. They looked forward to a time when there would be a perfect king, a perfect society, perfect peace among the nations, and perfect harmony throughout God's creation. Swords would be beaten into plowshares; the wolf would lie down with the lamb; war would be unthinkable; and justice, righteousness, mercy and the knowledge of the Lord would be the norm. Over such a perfect society, a shoot from the stump of Jesse would reign as the Wonder-Counselor, the Prince of Peace (Is 2:1–4; 9:2–7; 11:1–9).

As was the case during Israel's past, so in its messianic future, certain charismatic individuals would serve as agents of salvation. In this future age, the Spirit will rest upon an extraordinary king:

> *But a shoot shall sprout from the stump of Jesse,*
>   *and from his roots a bud shall blossom.*
> *The spirit of the LORD shall rest upon him:*
>   *a spirit of wisdom and of understanding,*
> *A spirit of counsel and of strength,*
>   *a spirit of knowledge and of fear of the LORD,*
>   *and his delight shall be the fear of the LORD.* (Is 11:1–3)

and on the mysterious Servant of the Lord:

> *Here is my servant whom I uphold,*
>> *my chosen one with whom I am pleased,*
> *upon whom I have put my spirit. . . .* (Isa 42:1)

and on the unidentified prophet who announces and describes the age to come:

> *The spirit of the LORD God is upon me,*
>> *because the LORD has anointed me;*
>> *He has sent me to bring glad tidings to the lowly,*
>> *to heal the brokenhearted,*
> *To proclaim liberty to the captives*
>> *and release to the prisoners,*
> *To announce a year of favor to the LORD*
>> *and a day of vindication to our God,*
>> *to comfort all who mourn.* (Is 61:1–2)

This messianic age will be marked by a general outpouring of the Spirit and a regeneration of *all* of the people:

> *I will pour out my spirit upon your offspring,*
>> *and my blessing upon your descendants.* (Is 44:3)

Probably the most striking description of this universal outpouring of the Spirit is the well-known passage from the prophet Joel:

> *And it shall come to pass afterward,*
>> *that I will pour out my spirit on all flesh;*
> *your sons and your daughters shall prophesy,*
>> *your old men shall dream dreams,*
>> *and your young men shall see visions.*
> *Even upon the men servants and maidservants,*
>> *in those days, I will pour out my spirit.* (Jl 3:1–2)

In this messianic age, the Spirit will no longer be given only to specific individuals, for a specific period of time, in order to perform some specific function. Rather, *all* flesh will receive the Spirit—both the men and the women; both the old and the young; both those who are free and those who are in servitude. This is an astonishing statement from an androcentric, patriarchal society that normally gives preference to the elders and free-born or freed men. This messianic vision is of an age when all will be inspirited, all will be charismatic.

Jesus, the Charismatic Fulfillment of Messianic Expectation

The account of the ministry of Jesus begins with his baptism by John. As reported in each of the Synoptic Gospels, it contains an allusion to the message of Isaiah 42 quoted above. In each version (Mt 3:13–17; Mk 1:9–11; Lk 3:21–22), the spirit descended upon Jesus, whom the voice calls "son." In the Greek version of Isaiah, *pais*, the word for "servant," can also be translated "son." This might explain the easy appropriation of the Isaian reference by the Christian author. Thus, the Gospels suggest that from the very beginning of his ministry, Jesus was the long-awaited messianic servant of the Lord.

Other gospel stories make further reference to the messianic character of the ministry of Jesus. When John the Baptist was in prison, he heard of Jesus' wondrous works, and he sent his disciples to discover whether or not Jesus was in fact "the one who is to come."

> *Jesus said to them in reply, "Go and tell John what you hear and see: the blind regain their sight, the lame walk, lepers are cleansed, the deaf hear, the dead are raised, and the poor have the good news proclaimed to them."* (Mt 11:4–5)

His response contains overtones of the messianic signs found in Isaiah:

> *Then will the eyes of the blind be opened,*
> *   the ears of the deaf be cleared;*
> *Then will the lame leap like a stag,*
> *   then the tongue of the dumb will sing.* (Is 35:5–6)

In a second story, this time from the Gospel of Luke, Jesus returns to Nazareth and is invited to read in the synagogue on the Sabbath. He selects the messianic passage from Isaiah 61, reads it, and then announces:

"Today this scripture passage is fulfilled in your hearing." (Lk 4:21)

These two gospel stories, each in its own way, imply that Jesus is a messianic figure. The first characterizes him as the mysterious Isaian servant of the Lord, the second as the unidentified prophet who announces and describes the age to come. Together they paint a portrait of a gentle, tender, and compassionate servant whose ministry is one of healing, consoling, and caring for all those in need. Such a ministry embodies the role of the judge (to deliver or to save), the king (to rule or to guide), and the prophet (to announce the saving word of God).

With the appearance of Jesus, the day of eschatological fulfillment has dawned. The time of Jesus was a time of healing and of blessing. It was the time of the Spirit as spoken of in the prophecy of Joel. It was the time of Pentecost:

When the time for Pentecost was fulfilled, they were all in one place together . . . And they were all filled with the holy Spirit . . . Then Peter stood up with the Eleven, raised his voice, and proclaimed to them, . . . "this is what was spoken through the prophet Joel" (Acts 2:1, 4, 14, 16).

In this way the messianic age has dawned, and we are living in its light.

Christian Ministry

Any consideration of Christian ministry must necessarily begin with an investigation of the stories about Jesus, since all ministries of the Christian church claim to be ministries of Christ. A fundamental characteristic of such ministry is the characteristic of service. Indeed, the very word that we translate as "ministry" is the Greek *diakonia*, meaning "service." The gospel narratives show that Jesus set himself as the model of service:

Just so, the Son of Man did not come to be served but to serve and to give his life as a ransom for many. (Mt 20:28, cf. Mk 10:45)

. . . I am among you as one who serves. (Lk 22:27)

In its own unique way, each Gospel shows him serving and instructing his followers to do the same:

Whoever wishes to be great among you shall be your servant; whoever wishes to be first among you shall be your slave. (Mt 20:26–27; cf. Mk 10:44)

In other Christian writings, the word *diakonia* is applied first to the material services necessary for the survival of the community, such as serving at table (Acts 6:1–4) and collecting money for the poor in Jerusalem (Acts 11:29; 12:25; Rom 15:31; 1 Cor 16:15; 2 Cor 8:4; 9:1, 12). It also has a broader meaning, as seen in the Letters of Paul:

Since we have gifts that differ according to the grace given to us, let us exercise them: if prophecy, in proportion to the faith; if ministry, in ministering; if one is a teacher, in teaching; if one exhorts, in exhortation; if one contributes, in generosity; if one is over others, with diligence; if one does acts of mercy, with cheerfulness. (Rom 12:6–8)

The various charismatic gifts that through faith and baptism Christians receive from the Spirit are clearly destined for use within the community. All Christians must realize the social character of their God-given talents or gifts and must employ them without jealousy or envy. These gifts that Paul lists in the passage from the Letter to the Romans are not necessarily miraculous. He seems to refer to *prophecy* as primarily preaching about religious matters. The second gift, *ministry*, refers to the management of material aid and the distribution of alms. *Teaching* is here clearly distinguished from preaching and service in the early Church. *Exhortation* is the guidance given by the spiritual leader of the community. The fifth gift is possessed by those who share their wealth. They are expected to do so with generous simplicity. Their gift of *philanthropy* differs from generosity because it is the dispensation of private wealth rather than common goods. The sixth gift of *diligence* belongs to those who are officials or administrators of the community. If the order of these charisms is significant, than the place of this kind of leadership is noteworthy. The last gift on this particular list belongs to those who perform *acts of mercy.*

Another list of ministerial gifts is found in Paul's First Letter to the Corinthians:

> *There are different kinds of spiritual gifts but the same Spirit; there are different forms of service but the same Lord; there are different workings but the same God who produces all of them in everyone. To each individual the manifestation of the Spirit is given for some benefit. To one is given through the Spirit the expression of wisdom; to another the expression of knowledge according to the same Spirit; to another faith by the same Spirit; to another gifts of healing according to the one Spirit; to another mighty deeds; to another prophecy; to another discernment of spirits; to another varieties of tongues; to another interpretation of tongues. But one and the same Spirit produces all of these, distributing them individually to each person as [the Spirit] wishes.*
> (1 Cor 12:4–11)

A close look at this letter will show that Paul's teaching on gifts and ministries is a faithful development of the messianic tradition. Paul's main concern is neither to defend nor to explain the gifts and ministries, but to exhort the Christians to unity amidst this diversity of Spirit-filled manifestations. He insists that Christian activity is not one unique and uniform experience separated from all other aspects of life. Nor is it opposed to material or intellectual pursuits.

Neither this list nor the one found in Romans is meant to be all inclusive. They contain samples of the kinds of gifts and abilities present and operative in the community. An exaggeration of one talent to the exclusion of another was probably at the heart of some of the rivalry in Corinth. Paul acknowledged the validity of all gifts, and he put their use and importance in proper perspective. He concludes his instruction about their value with a chapter describing the greatest of all gifts—

love. Still, insistence on the importance of love does not minimize the worth of other gifts and ministries. They are all ways through which the saving action of God is made present in our midst.

And so we come to our day, our age, our time. *This* is the time of the Spirit. *This* is the time of Pentecost. The Spirit of the Lord, that manifestation of the dynamic power of the divine, has been conferred upon each of us. As with the judges, the kings, the prophets of ancient Israel, and the early Christians, those who receive the Spirit are thus commissioned to act within the community in a charismatic manner. Qualities necessary to fulfill our mission have been conferred upon us. The Spirit has been given to us for the good of the community, not merely for our own benefit. Filled with the Spirit, we too are instruments by which the power of God can be communicated. Ours is a ministry of salvation and regeneration. It is a continuation of the ministry of Jesus who left us the Spirit that we might live fully.

Suggested Reading

Ackroyd, P. *Studies in the Religious Tradition of the Old Testament.* London: SCM, 1987.

Albertz, Rainer. *A History of Israelite Religion in the Old Testament Period.* London: SCM, 1994.

Blenkinsopp, J. *Sage, Priest, Prophet: Religious and Intellectual Leadership in Ancient Isreal.* Louisville, Ky.: Westminster/ John Knox, 1995.

Clements, R. E., ed. *The World of Ancient Israel: Sociological, Anthropological and Political Perspectives.* Cambridge, U.K.: Cambridge University Press, 1989.

de Vaux, R. *Ancient Israel: Its Life and Institutions.* London: Darton, Longman & Todd, 1961.

Grabbe, L. L. *Priests, Prophets, Diviners, Sages: A Socio-Historical Study of Religious Specialists in Ancient Israel.* Valley Forge, Pa.: Trinity Press International, 1995.

Wilson, R. *Prophecy and Society in Ancient Israel.* Philadelphia: Fortress, 1980.

Lay People and Church Governance: Oxymoron or Opportunity BY REV. JOHN BEAL, J.C.D.

Although the participation of lay people in the Church's teaching and sanctifying missions has received considerable attention, not so much attention has been given to the participation by lay people in the Church's governing mission. This paper begins with an overview of the consultative roles open to lay people in the governance of dioceses and parishes and explains the role of consultation in ecclesial governance. It then explains the governance roles open to lay people by appointment to ecclesiastical offices. It examines the controverted question of whether lay people can be delegated to exercise ecclesiastical power of governance or jurisdiction and concludes that they can be so delegated.

Introduction

Echoing the teaching of the Second Vatican Council, canon 204, §1 of the revised Latin *Code of Canon Law* acknowledges that all of the faithful, ordained and nonordained alike, "have become sharers in Christ's priestly, prophetic and royal office in their own manner." The reforms that followed the council and have now been incorporated into the revised code opened wide the door for a wide variety of forms of participation by lay people in the Church's sanctifying and teaching missions. However, the door to participation in the Church's governance mission has remained only slightly ajar.

Several factors help to account for the slow pace with which lay people have been incorporated into governance roles in the Church. The centuries-long struggle to secure the Church's freedom from the embrace of secular magnates that began with the investiture controversy of the eleventh and twelfth centuries left church leaders leery of anything that smacked of "lay jurisdiction."[1] In the United States, the trusteeship conflict of the nineteenth century left a bitter aftertaste of suspicion of lay involvement in church governance.[2] These struggles generated negative attitudes toward lay participation in church governance that were not easily dislodged by the *novus habitus mentis* called for by the council's teaching. Moreover, the conciliar teaching itself sparked a heated canonico-theological debate about the nature of the power of governance and the possibility of lay people sharing in it.[3] As long as these doctrinal issues remain unresolved, many otherwise sympathetic bishops and pastors have been reluctant to appoint lay people to positions involving governance.

Despite these causes for hesitation, the conciliar teaching on the suitability of lay people to "be called to a more immediate cooperation in the apostolate of the hierarchy"[4] and even, when ordained ministers were lacking, to be entrusted with "some of [their] sacred offices in so far as they can"[5] was not ignored. The post-conciliar era has seen the creation (or, in some cases, the recovery) of consultative bodies to give lay people a voice in the governance of the Church, the opening to lay people of a variety of ecclesiastical offices previously reserved to the clergy, and the emergence of new positions that involve responsibility for pastoral direction and leadership and that are open to lay people. Although these developments have occurred, to greater or lesser degrees, at all levels of the Church, this paper focuses on lay participation in church governance at the parish and diocesan levels.

The paper will look first at opportunities for lay people to play consultative roles in diocesan and parish governance. It will then offer some reflections on the variety of roles in ecclesial decision making and the significance of consultation for church governance. The paper will turn to directive roles open to lay people in diocesan and parish governance. It will then examine the controverted question of the possibility of granting lay ecclesial ministers some share in ecclesiastical power of governance. It will conclude with some reflections on challenges to effective incorporation of lay people in the Church's governing mission.

LAY PARTICIPATION IN GOVERNANCE: CONSULTATIVE ROLES

Structures for Consultation in the 1983 *Code of Canon Law.*

The code recognizes the right of the faithful "to make known their needs, especially spiritual ones, and desires" and to communicate "their opinion on matters which pertain to the good of the Church" to church leaders and to other members of the faithful (c. 212, §§2–3). To this right of the faithful to a respectful expression of their views corresponds an obligation of church authorities to give these expressions of needs, desires, and opinions a respectful hearing.[6] These rights belong to the faithful as individuals, but many members of the faithful may lack the opportunities, resources, or skills needed to exercise these rights effectively. Consequently, the law provides for a variety of consultative bodies at the diocesan and parochial levels to structure the expression of needs, desires, and opinions and to ensure that the voice of lay people will not be absent from ecclesial decision-making processes.[7]

The code itself either requires or recommends the participation of lay people in a variety of bodies, some with a long canonical pedigree and others of a more recent vintage. Some lay people must be called to a diocesan synod[8] (c. 463, §1, 5°). The code mandates that every diocese have a finance council (c. 492, §1). Although the code does not require that lay people serve on this council, in fact lay people are more likely than clergy to have the expertise "in financial matters as well as civil law" required for this office.[9] The diocesan bishop may also establish a diocesan pastoral council "whose responsibility it is to investigate under the authority of the diocesan bishop all those things which pertain to pastoral works, to ponder them and to propose practical conclusions about them" (c. 511). Although the membership of the pastoral council is mixed, it is to include "especially lay persons" (c. 512, §1).

Each parish must have a finance council to "aid the pastor in the administration of parish goods" (c. 537), and the diocesan bishop can mandate that each parish have a pastoral council to "help in fostering pastoral activity" (c. 536, §1).[10] Specification of the membership and responsibilities of these parish-level councils is left largely to particular law. However, the law presumes that most, if not all, members of these parish councils will be lay people.

In addition to these diocesan and parish councils expressly mentioned in the code, many dioceses have created other consultative bodies and processes for dealing with particular areas and issues. Thus, lay people serve as members of diocesan and parish school boards and advisory boards for Catholic charities and as trustees of Catholic colleges, hospitals, and other institutional apostolates. In addition, many dioceses have involved lay people in structured consultative processes prior to the closure or merger of parishes, the establishment or suppression of Catholic schools, the renovation of churches, and other decisions with a significant impact on the life of the community.[11]

The Role of Consultation in Church Governance

Despite these opportunities for lay involvement in ecclesial decision making, critics often point out that, with the exception of a few cases involving the diocesan—and possibly the parish—finance council, the lay people on these councils and boards have a role that is "merely consultative," while decision-making power remains exclusively the prerogative of the diocesan bishop or the pastor. While this criticism is accurate, it betrays a rather impoverished understanding of decision-making processes that reduces a very complex process to the right or power to make the ultimate choice of a course of action. However, as Robert Kennedy has pointed out, "the making of a choice is only one element in decision making, and not always the most important or the most influential."[12]

It is true that canon law accords lay people—as individuals, as communities, and as members of consultative bodies—little choice-making authority. However, they can and do have broad opportunities for sharing responsibility for ecclesial decision making with their bishops and pastors through their generation of alternative strategies, assembly of information, and implementation and evaluation of choices.[13] Despite its reservation of most choice-making authority to bishops and pastors, the code evidences a strong preference for collaborative rather than unilateral decision making.[14] This underlying emphasis on consultative governance in the revised code is consistent with the course set in the documents of the Second Vatican Council, but it is in sharp contrast with the prevailing tendency of canon law from the Gregorian Reform through the regime of the 1917 code.[15]

This marked change in emphasis is the result of the shift, dictated by the ecclesiology of Vatican II, in the central focus of the Church's law from the clerical hierarchy to the Christian faithful.[16] As sharers in the threefold *munera* of Christ and the Church in virtue of their baptisms, the lay Christian faithful are "the indispensable collaborators and necessary interlocutors of the activity of the pastors."[17] A consultative role for the lay Christian faithful is a concrete way of articulating for the domain of church governance the reciprocal relationship that exists between the common priesthood of all the faithful and the ministerial priesthood. Thus, consulting the faithful in matters of governance is not only an effective management technique but also a demand of ecclesial communion.

> *The role of the common priesthood (and of the* sensus fidei) *is not to help the ministerial priesthood but to express its own witness and its own views on the faith and on church discipline. The common priesthood is in fact primary, even in relationship to the ministerial priesthood. Consequently the latter cannot ignore the witness of the former without violating the principle of communion. Although the deliberative vote and the consultative vote are institutions that do not succeed in translating into juridical terms the full ecclesiological dynamics of* communio hierarchica, *they are in fact the most transparent and therefore least inadequate technical means of expressing it.*[18]

The principle of communion can be violated equally by management styles that eschew consultation or treat it as an empty formality for reaching a foreordained conclusion and by attitudes that reduce having a meaningful voice in decisions to having a deliberative vote.

LAY PEOPLE IN GOVERNANCE: DIRECTIVE ROLES

The Notion of Ecclesiastical Office

The participation of lay people in the governance of dioceses and parishes is not restricted to their having a voice—either as individuals or as members of consultative bodies—in ecclesial decision making. Also open to lay people are certain diocesan and parish leadership positions that entail some share in the function of governance. Some of these ministerial positions meet the canonical criteria for ecclesiastical offices, that is, they are functions "constituted in a stable manner by divine or ecclesiastical law to be exercised for a spiritual purpose" (c. 145, §1).

The existence of an ecclesiastical office is not determined by whether it involves a full-time or a part-time position or whether the person receives a salary or is a volunteer. The hallmarks of an ecclesiastical office are the continuance of the function in question beyond the tenure of any individual who carries it out, its institutionalization in church law, and its destination to a spiritual purpose. The code has established some ministerial functions in dioceses and parishes as ecclesiastical offices; particular law can establish others as ecclesiastical offices. Even if a function or a position is not explicitly designated as an "ecclesiastical office" in the law that establishes it, it is an office as long as it meets the criteria of canon 145. The preference of many dioceses in the United States for issuing "policies" and "guidelines" instead of promulgating "particular laws" can make it especially difficult to determine whether they have, in fact, established ministerial positions as ecclesiastical offices.[19]

The issue of whether certain functions have been constituted as ecclesiastical offices is not merely academic. Establishment of a function as an ecclesiastical office recognizes the importance of the function for the life of the Church and for the relative permanence of the community's need for this ministry. Its establishment as an office requires the intervention of competent ecclesiastical authority, which gives the function a public role in the life of the Church. In a diocese, this competent authority is usually the diocesan bishop, who also enjoys the right to confer the office unless some other method for its provision is specified in the law (c. 148). The competent authority can also set qualifications for the reception of an office established by particular law and add qualifications to those established by universal law (c. 149, §1).

In addition to enjoying official recognition of the importance of their ministries and their qualifications, office holders enjoy a certain measure of stability in office or job security. Office holders can be removed only for cause (cc.193–194). Before issuing a decree of removal, the competent authority is to hear the affected person (c. 50). The decree itself must be in writing and must contain at least a summary of the reasons for the removal (c. 51). Moreover, if the office is the source of the office holder's livelihood, he or she is entitled to reasonable severance pay on removal (c. 195).

Lay People and Ecclesiastical Offices

At the Parish Level. Ecclesiastical offices and functions can be conferred on qualified lay people unless the law reserves particular offices to those who are ordained (c. 228, §1). Canon 150 reserves to priests offices "entailing the full care of souls, for whose fulfillment the exercise of the priestly order is required." Thus, a lay person can be neither the pastor of a parish (c. 521, §1) nor a parochial vicar (c. 546) nor a member of the presbyteral "team" entrusted with the pastoral care of a parish *in solidum* (c. 517, §1). However, when there is a shortage of presbyters, a lay person can be entrusted by the diocesan bishop with the pastoral care of a parish. In this latter case, the bishop is also to appoint a "priest endowed with the powers and faculties of a pastor to supervise the pastoral care" (c. 517, §2). Although the code foresees the entrusting of the pastoral care of parishes to lay persons only in situations where there is a "dearth of priests" (*sacerdotum penuriam*), the use of this phrase elsewhere in the code suggests that canon 517, §2 entails not a temporary deputation but a new form of ministry to deal with a long-term problem.[20] Thus, the new ministry of the lay person entrusted with the pastoral care of a parish has the stability required for it to be considered an ecclesiastical office.

There is already some experience with the implementation of canon 517, §2, and some particular law that attempts to spell out the rights and responsibilities of this new office and to define lines of account-ability.[21] Nevertheless, this particular law is still tentative and, at times, flawed,[22] and the experience has not yet been subjected to critical scru-tiny. Thus, this opening in the law for a diocesan bishop to entrust the pastoral care of a parish to a lay person affords an opportunity for both creative implementation and careful reflection on the prospects and pit-falls of ecclesial lay ministry.[23]

In situations where a resident pastor is responsible for a parish, the code itself establishes no offices or ministries of leadership for lay people at the parish level, except for membership on parish pastoral and finance councils. However, particular law and, more frequently, local practice have given rise to a number of leadership positions that have a pro-nounced governance dimension. Under the authority of the pastor, principals of parish schools and parish directors of religious education are responsible for recruiting and retaining teachers and catechists, implementing educational programs, and making decisions that affect students' rights to receive or continue to receive Catholic education and, at times, to receive certain sacraments. Some parishes have given business managers a share in the pastor's responsibility for the admin-istration of the temporal goods of the parish. Whether these positions are ecclesiastical offices or simply stable ministries depends on whether they have received formal recognition in law. Nevertheless, they repre-sent a significant form of sharing by lay people in the governance role of the pastor.

In addition to these offices or ministerial positions with clear gover-nance implications at the parish level, many lay ecclesial ministers exercise leadership roles in parishes that transcend the areas of respon-sibility suggested by their titles and job descriptions. Lay "pastoral ministers" (titles are diverse but these ministers often assume many of the functions assigned to parochial vicars in another era), youth minis-ters, and other members of the "parish staff" (or the "parish team" in the broad sense of the term) can have an important and, at times, criti-cal role in parish decision making when the pastor has adopted a collaborative style of leadership. However, these ministerial positions are usually not ecclesiastical offices in the canonical sense, and the role of these parish ministers in decision making is usually not formally structured but is based on informal and personal relationships. As a result, the positions themselves lack stability, and the ministers' voices in decision making are dependent on the managerial style of the pastor.

At the Diocesan Level. The revised code has opened most offices in the judicial section of the diocesan curia to qualified lay men and women. Lay persons can serve as tribunal notaries (c. 483, §2), advocates (c. 1483), auditors (c. 1428, §2), defenders of the bond, promoters of justice (c. 1435), and—as members of colleges including two clerics—judges (c. 1421, §2). The only tribunal office reserved to a priest is that of judicial vicar (c. 1420, §4). However, many tribunals in the United States have appointed lay persons to the position of "tribunal director" to carry out many of the functions of the judicial vicar in virtue of delegation either from the diocesan bishop or from the judicial vicar.

In the administrative section of the diocesan curia, lay people are barred by law from being appointed as vicars general or episcopal vicars (c. 478, §1). The code also requires that a priest hold the optional office of moderator of the curia, whose responsibility is "to coordinate the exercise of administrative responsibilities and to see to it that the other members of the curia duly fulfill the office entrusted to them" (c. 473, §2). Nevertheless, many dioceses have reserved the title "vicar" for those priests who exercise a role of oversight and coordination in territorial regions of the diocese and have assigned responsibility for substantive areas of ministry (e.g., education, social service, religious, campus ministry, family life) to clerics or lay people under a variety of titles (e.g., diocesan directors, secretaries, coordinators, delegates). While this terminological sleight of hand allows these positions to be opened to lay people, it does not avoid the question of whether these lay ministers can exercise by delegation the authority over these areas of ministry that an episcopal vicar would have in virtue of office.

In addition to service as members of the diocesan finance council and the diocesan pastoral council, the code opens to lay people the offices of diocesan chancellor (c. 483, §2) and diocesan finance officer (c. 494, §1). Although the code treats the chancellor as the senior notary and archivist of the diocese,[24] it has been the custom in the United States to invest the chancellor by delegation with most of the powers the vicar general enjoys in virtue of office. The finance officer has, in virtue of office, extensive authority over the day-to-day management of the temporalities of the diocese and can be invested with other powers ordinarily reserved to the diocesan bishop (c. 494, §§3–4; 1278).

The diocesan curia of the typical diocese in the United States is rarely as spartan as the one sketched in the code.[25] Particular law and organizational documents have created a variety of offices to deal with religious education, Catholic schools, religious, charities, communications, and a host of other areas of pastoral concern. Key positions in these offices are usually open to qualified lay people and involve significant roles in the shaping of diocesan policy; deployment of personnel and other diocesan resources; hiring, supervision, and retention of other ministers and employees at both the diocesan and the parish levels; and implementation and evaluation of programs and policies. While it may seem oxymoronic to speak of a ministry of bureaucracy, various lay officials of the diocesan curia do exercise such a ministry and, in doing so, have a directive role in diocesan governance.

LAY PEOPLE AND THE POWER OF GOVERNANCE

Offices Requiring Power of Governance

The inevitable question, of course, is whether these lay ecclesial ministers who have directive functions at the parish and diocesan levels can or do exercise ecclesiastical power of governance or jurisdiction. Canon 274, §1 stipulates: "Only clerics can obtain those offices for whose exercise there is required the power of orders or the power of ecclesiastical governance." At first glance, this reservation seems to exclude lay people from most significant roles in ecclesial governance. However, while the offices of vicar general, episcopal vicar, and judicial vicar entail the exercise of power of governance and are reserved to priests, relatively few of the other offices mentioned in the code require the exercise of power of governance. Moreover, the code itself is not entirely consistent in excluding lay people from offices entailing the exercise of power of governance. For example, the ecclesiastical offices of diocesan judge[26] and diocesan finance officer[27] entail the exercise of power of governance, but both are open to lay people (c. 1421, §2 and c. 494, §1).

The Question of Delegation: Conflicting Opinions

The reservation of most offices entailing the power of governance to clerics does not necessarily and of itself preclude lay people from exercising that power in virtue of delegation.[28]

The possibility of giving lay people a share in the exercise of power of governance or jurisdiction has been a hotly disputed issue since the close of the council. One side in this debate holds that the power of jurisdiction is so intimately connected to the power of orders that only the ordained are capable of having and exercising jurisdiction.[29] The other side holds that the power of jurisdiction is a power distinct from that of orders, which can be shared with and exercised by those who are not ordained.[30] While much of this debate has been phrased in the somewhat arcane terminology of canon law, it is an ecclesiological debate in the last analysis.

Lay People Cannot Exercise Power of Governance. The theological rationales of those who maintain that lay people cannot be given a share in the power of governance differ, sometimes markedly, but they have a common starting point. All of them insist that in *Lumen Gentium*, §21 *et passim*, and in its *Nota explicativa praevia*, the Second Vatican Council reversed nearly a millennium of canonical tradition and taught that there is but one sacred power *(una sacra potestas)* in the Church. Some (Bertrams and the later Corecco) hold that this one sacred power is radically and substantially conferred by sacred ordination, even though the *munera* of teaching and governing can be exercised only in hierarchical communion or with a canonical mission. Others (Mörsdorf and most of the Munich school) hold that the powers of orders and governance are materially and formally distinct dimensions of the one sacred power, but that these two dimensions are so inextricably intertwined that they cannot be exercised or even exist independently. Thus, even the celebration of the eucharist entails exercise of the power of governance because it involves presiding over a community of the faithful, and enactment of legislation implicates the power of orders since all law in the Church is in the service of the supreme law—the *salus animarum*. According to either approach, sharing power of governance with lay people is not only juridically prohibited but ontologically impossible.

All of those who deny that lay people can share in the power of governance emphasize the essential difference asserted in *Lumen Gentium* §10 between the common priesthood of all the faithful and the ministerial priesthood of the ordained. What distinguishes the ministerial priesthood from the common priesthood is the sacred power conferred on the latter by ordination that enables them to proclaim the word and to celebrate the sacraments *in persona Christi*. Through word and sacrament, participants in the ministerial priesthood continue Christ's ministry of building up the Church as a reality that is at once a visible society and an invisible spiritual communion.

Although they use a variety of imagery to describe the Church, they articulate the difference between the common and the ministerial priesthoods primarily in terms of a mystical body ecclesiology that some have described as "Christo-monistic."[31] Participants in the common priesthood represent and make visible Christ's body, and participants in the ministerial priesthood represent and make visible Christ the head of the body.[32] So central is this contrast between the common priesthood/body of Christ and the ministerial priesthood/representation of Christ the head that the very sacramentality of the Church depends on it. Mörsdorf insists:

> *The sacramental sign capacity of the Church is bound to the Church's own hierarchical structure; i.e., the Church is a sign of salvation only when the Lord, its invisible head, is represented visibly through men. Without a visible head the Church cannot be a visible representation of the Lord's love. The hierarchical structure of the Church is based on the will of the Lord to continue his saving work through authorized representatives of the Church.*[33]

Thus, exclusion of lay people from the exercise of sacred power is required for the sake of the integrity of the Church as a *sacramentum salutis.*

Lay People Can Exercise Power of Governance. Despite the significant differences of approach and perspective among them, protagonists of the possibility of sharing power of governance with lay people also share a common point of departure. They all accept in principle the position—traditional in the West during most of the Church's second millennium—that the powers of orders and jurisdiction, while ultimately rooted in Christ, are distinct both in their natures and in their manner of transmission. The power of orders is conferred by sacramental ordination; the power of jurisdiction by canonical mission. The essential distinction of the two powers entails that there is no *a priori* reason why they cannot exist and be exercised separately as has often occurred in the history of the Church, most notably in cases of nonbishops elected as pope between their elections and their episcopal ordinations.

Supporters of the possibility of sharing power of governance with lay people acknowledge the essential distinction between the common and ministerial priesthoods, but they tend to emphasize that these two forms of participation in the one priesthood of Christ are, as *Lumen Gentium* §10 also taught, ordered to one another *(ad invicem tamen ordinantur).* They tend to articulate the reciprocal interrelatedness of the common and ministerial priesthood in terms of an ecclesiology of *communio* that situates ordained ministry squarely within the community of believers instead of emphasizing its over-againstness. Their various ecclesiologies of *communio* have a pronounced pneumatological dimension. Thus, they tend to emphasize the commissioning of all the faithful for ministry in the Church and in the world through baptism and confirmation and the role of charisms in the building up of the Church.

As a result, "ministeriality" is a note of the Church itself and not merely of an elite cadre within it. From the heart of this ministerial Church, some members of the faithful are called forth and are commissioned through sacramental ordination to serve the edification of the Church by an exercise of the *munera* of teaching, sanctifying, and governing in a way essentially different than that proper to other members of the Christian faithful. Just as the ministries of word and sacrament closely intertwine and converge in the ministry of the ordained, so the powers of orders and jurisdiction are necessarily joined in the offices of the Roman pontiff for the universal Church, of the diocesan bishop for the particular church, and of the pastor for the local community. However, like the ministries of word and sacrament, these powers are distinct and can be exercised separately. Thus, there is no obstacle in principle to these office holders sharing some of their governance power with other members of the faithful—lay or ordained—when the good of the Church suggests its necessity or usefulness. Indeed, sharing power of governance with competent lay people can be seen as an official recognition of the charisms of leadership they possess.

The Question of Delegation: the 1983 *Code of Canon Law*

Since protagonists of both of these irreconcilable theories cite different strands of the ecclesiology of Vatican II as authority in support of their positions, it was inevitable that their debate would spill out of academe and into the process of revising the *Code of Canon Law*. The result of the sometimes heated discussions during the code revision process is canon 129:

> *§1. In accord with the prescriptions of law, those who have received sacred orders are capable of* (habiles sunt) *the power of governance, which exists in the Church by divine institution and is also called the power of jurisdiction.*

> *§2. Lay members of the Christian faithful can cooperate* (cooperari possunt) *in the exercise of this power in accord with the norm of law.*[34]

Although both sides of the debate claim to find vindication for their positions in this canon,[35] the fact is that canon 129 is a pragmatic compromise designed to allow the Church to carry on its governance activity until a consensus on the underlying theoretical and doctrinal issues can be reached.

An Interpretation of Canon 129. Determining whether this pragmatic compromise leaves room for diocesan bishops and pastors to share their own power of governance with lay people through the institute of delegation requires a careful canonical analysis of canon 129. The code itself provides the principles for the interpretation of its laws. Canon 17 stipulates:

> *Ecclesiastical laws are to be understood in accord with the proper meaning of the words considered in their text and context. If the meaning remains doubtful and obscure, recourse is to be taken to parallel passages, if such exist, to the purpose and circumstances of the law, and to the mind of the legislator.*

In addition, laws that restrict the free exercise of rights "are subject to a strict interpretation," that is, to the narrowest construction consistent with the literal meaning of the words of the norm (c. 18). Since canon 129 impinges on the freedom of diocesan bishops and other ecclesiastical authorities in their choice of collaborators in the ministry of governance, it must be interpreted in the way least restrictive of their discretion. The interpretation of canon 129 hinges on the proper understanding of two critical terms: *habiles* and *cooperari.*

Habiles—Some have argued that by designating the ordained as *habiles* for the power of governance canon, 129, §1 implicitly identifies lay people as *inhabiles* for exercising this power. Jaeger claims: "The logical rule of discourse: *'inclusio unius est exclusio alterius'* means that this capacity is exclusive to those who are in holy orders, exclusive that is of those who are not."[36] The conclusion may seem logical, but it is inconsistent with the stricture of canon 10 that only those laws that expressly declare a person *inhabilis* for acting have that effect. The exclusion, if there is one, is not implicit but tacit. Nor is it consistent with the use of the term *habilis* elsewhere in the code. While the term is sometimes used to distinguish the *habiles* from the *inhabiles,*[37] it is also used simply to call attention to the suitability, aptness, or eligibility of particular persons for a given task.[38] For example, no one would claim that by designating lay people as *habiles* to receive a mandate to teach the sacred sciences,

c. 229, §3 meant to declare the ordained *inhabiles* to receive this mandate.

This nonexclusive sense of *habilis* was clearly the one in the mind of the members of the Code Commission who drafted the revised law. Although every schema of the revised law designated only the ordained as *habiles* for the power of governance, the drafters clearly intended to give lay people the possibility for a share in that power.[39] In fact, early in the revision process, the norms on the power of governance were moved from the section on clerics (where they had been in the 1917 code) to the section on general norms precisely because of the recognition that the power of governance is no longer an exclusively clerical preserve.[40] Thus, the designation of clerics as *habiles* for the power of governance simply calls attention to their special suitability for functions involving the power of governance; it does not disqualify lay people from performing those functions should the diocesan bishop deem it necessary or appropriate.

Cooperari—Those who maintain that the code withholds from lay people the possibility of any share in the power of governance argue that the use of the term *cooperari* in canon 129, §2 limits the role of lay people in church governance to consultative and merely administrative functions.[41] It is true that *cooperari* is not as strong as the phrase *eam partem habere*, which has been used to explain the share of lay people in power of governance in earlier drafts of the revised law. However, the usage of *cooperari* and its variants elsewhere in the code does not support the claim that it limits lay people to a merely consultative and ancillary role in the exercise of the power of governance.[42]

"Cooperation" is the term used to describe the working together of the diocesan bishop and the presbyterate to provide for the pastoral care of the particular church (c. 369) and parochial vicars are defined as *cooperatores* "with the pastor in common council and endeavor with him and also under his authority" (c. 545, §1). The "cooperation" of the presbyterate with the diocesan bishop and of parochial vicars with pastors is not a merely consultative and ancillary involvement in the bishops' and pastors' ministries. Rather, they "cooperate" by assuming many of the functions of bishops and pastors. Thus, presbyters and parochial vicars proclaim the word of God, gather communities for the celebration of the eucharist and other sacraments, and govern the communities or aspects of communities entrusted to them under the authority, respectively, of the diocesan bishop and pastor.

Canon 759 stipulates that lay people "can also be called upon to cooperate *(cooperentur)* with the bishops and presbyters in the exercise of the ministry of the word." Subsequent canons in Book III make clear that this cooperation of lay people in the ministry of the word includes preaching in churches and oratories under certain circumstances (c. 766) and providing catechetical formation (c. 776). One would hardly describe any of these forms of cooperation in the ministry of the word as merely consultative and ancillary. Thus, the words of canon 129 properly understood in their text and context support the proposition that lay people can have as real and substantive a share in the exercise of power of governance as they can in the ministry of the word.

Consequences for Ecclesial Governance. If this analysis of canon 129 is correct, then lay people can cooperate in the exercise of the power of governance as delegates of their pastors and diocesan bishops. In fact, as a private reply of a consultor of the Apostolic Signatura explained:

> Canon 129, §2 . . . is canonical teaching which seeks to explain why laity can exercise and do exercise the power of governing. When laity are called by the norm of law for cooperation in the exercise of power, the same norms and laws concerning the acquisition of power, its exercise, and the rest, are valid.[43]

Indeed, one can see a warrant for the delegation of episcopal authority to lay people within the code itself in canon 1278, which suggests that the diocesan bishop commit to the diocesan finance officer his authority to supervise the administration of the temporal goods of juridic persons subject to him and to appoint administrators for the goods of juridic persons when neither the law nor their charters contains another provision.

Although a diocesan bishop cannot validly delegate his legislative authority (c. 135, §2), the law places few restrictions on his freedom to delegate his executive authority. The critical criteria for such delegations are the competence of the proposed delegate for the task in question and the pastoral needs of the portion of the People of God entrusted to the bishop's care. There may be specific episcopal functions such as the concession to presbyters of the faculty to confirm and the faculty to hear confessions that are so priestly in character that they cannot be delegated to lay people.[44] Even in these areas, however, the bishop could utilize the traditional canonical institute of designation, that is, by his agreeing in advance to delegate whomever a lay official in the curia or in a parish designates to exercise these faculties.[45]

The institute of delegation gives the diocesan bishop broad discretion to share significant parts of his directive with lay people, coordinating supervisory and decision-making authority in the pastoral governance of the diocese. In fact, many bishops may have already done so. When a case involving a dispute between a teacher and a lay principal of Catholic school operated by a diocese was referred to the Apostolic Signatura, a consultor observed that, "although he does not receive the full power of the diocesan bishop, nevertheless [the lay principal] receives all of the faculties and offices necessary to moderate the school in the name of the bishop."[46] In other words, the lay principal shares by delegation in a subordinate and dependent way the diocesan bishop's governance power over the school.

If this is true, it is hard to escape the conclusion that, perhaps without realizing the fact, lay principals of Catholic schools, superintendents of schools, directors of religious education, business managers, and numerous other diocesan officials and parish ministers are already exercising power of governance in a subordinate and dependent way by virtue of delegation from the diocesan bishop or the pastor. Without diminishing or compromising their ultimate responsibility for the pastoral good of the portions of the People of God entrusted to their care, diocesan bishops and pastors can entrust to qualified lay people additional shares in their executive power of governance if such concessions will serve the good of souls.

Conclusion

As the number of ordained ministers declines and those available for ministry continue to age, diocesan bishops and pastors will feel increasingly the need to enlist the cooperation of lay people in their ministry of ecclesial governance—both as paid staff and as volunteers—in consultative and directive roles. As the complexity of issues and challenges facing the Church grows, bishops and pastors will need increasingly to turn for counsel to lay people who, at least in countries such as the United States, are often better educated than the clergy. The growing involvement of lay people in the ministry of ecclesial governance poses two particular challenges:

- articulating a coherent canonico-theological rationale that transcends the current doctrinal impasse about the participation of lay people in the exercise of power of governance; and
- making consultative bodies and processes effective vehicles for building consensus and facilitating decision making in the local church.

Since a primary purpose of the colloquium "Toward a Theology of Ecclesial Lay Ministry" is to lay the groundwork for the sort of canonico-theological framework that can transcend the current impasse, an attempt to address this challenge should await the outcome of the colloquium. However, a concluding reflection on the challenge of making consultative bodies and process effective in ecclesial governance seems appropriate.

Making consultative bodies and processes effective will require governance styles accommodated to providing pastoral leadership to a Catholic population that is well educated, independent-minded, and schooled in democratic mores. In this respect, Congar was prophetic when he observed that effective consultation seems to call, on the part of the clergy, for a very sincere effort at the various levels of ecclesial life, an effort that, if it creates its own difficulties in some circumstances, will nevertheless be effective. It means "putting the laity in the picture" and, honestly and without artifice, making them feel that they are there. To do that, they must not be approached as a matter of form, or in some other way that nobody would use if he wants to be understood and followed—the approach must be real. They must be told what is proposed, be given so far as possible the reasons for a decision made, and be informed about results, difficulties, and new measures required; thus may their agreement be obtained and their help be enlisted in the spreading of their clergy's aims and decisions. This way of going to work always gets results, and no other way does. It involves no indiscretions or imprudences, no derogation of authority. Relations between clergy and people are able to have that mutual confidence and loyalty—those exchanges of views and sharings of ideas, which, as everything shows, ought to distinguish the Lord's followers today as they distinguished the Church immediately after the Pasch and Pentecost.[47]

Effective consultation requires governance styles different than that of the imperial episcopacy (often emulated in their own domain by pastors) that prevailed in the United States throughout much of the Church's immigrant era. To adopt a governance style conducive to effective consultation is not to abdicate hierarchical authority or to democratize the Church. Rather, it is to recover the governance style of Cyprian of Carthage, who could both insist that nothing was to be done in the Church without the bishop and acknowledge that as bishop he did nothing *"sine consilio vestro et consensu plebis."*[48]

Notes

1. For a discussion of the Gregorian Reform as a struggle for the *libertas Ecclesiae* from secular (i.e., lay) jurisdiction, see Yves Congar, *L'Église de saint Augustin à l'époque moderne* (Paris: Les Éditions du Cerf, 1970), pp. 102–112. More generally see, Yves Congar, *Lay People in the Church: A Study for the Theology of the Laity* (Westminster, Md.: Newman Press, 1965), pp. 38–58.

2. For an exposition of the trusteeship controversy and its lingering impact on attitudes toward participation of lay people in church governance, see Patrick Carey, *People, Priests, and Prelates: Ecclesiastical Democracy and the Tensions of Trusteeism* (Notre Dame: University of Notre Dame Press, 1987).

3. For an overview of this post-conciliar discussion of the nature of ecclesiastical jurisdiction, see John P. Beal, "The Exercise of the Power of Governance by Lay People: State of the Question," *The Jurist* 55 (1995): 10–52.

4. *Lumen Gentium*, no. 33.

5. Ibid., no. 35.

6. See *Lumen Gentium*, no. 37 and Pontifical Commission on the Means of Social Communication, instruction *Communio et progressio*, January 29, 1971, nos. 115–116, 120: *AAS* 63 (1971): 634–636: "Since the Church is a living body, she needs public opinion in order to sustain a giving and taking between her members. Without this, she cannot advance in thought and action [As Pope Pius XII said:] 'Something would be lacking in her life if she had no public opinion. Both pastors of souls and lay people would be to blame for this.' Catholics should be fully aware of the real freedom to speak their minds which stems from a 'feeling for the faith' and from love. . . . Those who exercise authority in the Church will take care to ensure that there is a responsible exchange of freely held and expressed opinion among the People of God. More than this, they will set up norms and conditions for this to take place. . . . The normal flow of life and the smooth functioning of government within the Church require a steady two-way flow of information between the ecclesiastical authorities at all levels and the faithful as individuals and as organized groups." English translation in Austin Flannery, *Vatican Council II: The Conciliar and Post Conciliar Documents*, vol. I (Northport, N.Y.: Costello, 1981), nos. 330–332.

7. For an overview of the various consultative bodies in the particular church and their functions, see Juan Ignacio Arrieta, "Organos de participación y corresponsabilidad en la Iglesia diocesana," *Ius Canonicum* 34 (1994): 553–593; Frans Daneels, "De dioecesanis corresponsabilitatis organis," *Periodica* 74 (1985): 301–324; Michael Fahey, "Diocesan Governance in Modern Catholic Theology and in the 1983 *Code of Canon Law*," in *The Ministry of Governance*, James Mallett, ed. (Washington: CLSA, 1986): 121–139; Libero Gerosa, "Les conseils diocésains: structures 'synodales' et moments de 'co-responsabilité' dans le service pastoral," in *La Synodalité: La participation au gouvernement de l'Eglise. Actes du VII congres international de droit canonique, L'Année canonique*, hors serie (1992), 2:781–795; Filippo Giannini, "La Chiesa particolare e gli organismi di partecipazione," *Apollinaris* 56 (1983): 514–527; James Provost, "The Working Together of Consultative

Bodies—Great Expectations?" *The Jurist* 40 (1980): 257–281; Giuseppe Spinelli, "Organismi di partecipazione nella struttura della Chiesa locale," in *The New Code of Canon Law: Proceedings of the Fifth International Congress of Canon Law*, Michel Thériault and Jean Thorn, eds. (Ottawa: Saint Paul University, 1986), 2:627–634.

8. For a practical discussion of the diocesan synod, see Ann Rehrauer, OSF, "Diocesan Synods," *CLSA Proceedings* 49 (1987): 1–15. For more technical discussion of the diocesan synod, see Jean Beyer, "De synodo dioecesano," *Periodica* 81 (1992): 381–423; Silvio Ferrari, "I Sinodi diocesani del post-concilio," *Revista Española de Derecho Canonico* 46 (1989): 179–187; Gianfranco Ghirlanda, "Il sinodo diocesano," in *Ius in Vita et in Missione Ecclesiae: Acta Symposii Internationalis Iuris Canonici*, ed. Pontificium Consilium de Legum Textibus Interpretandis (Vatican City: Typis Polyglottis Vaticanis, 1994), 577–592; Lawrence Jennings, "A Renewed Understanding of the Diocesan Synod," *Studia canonica* 20 (1986): 319–354; Roch Pagé, "Les synodes diocésains: expériences et perspectives," in La Synodalité, 2:619–628; James Provost, "The Ecclesiological Nature and Function of the Diocesan Synod in the Real Life of the Church, *La Synodalité*, 2:537–558; David Ross, "The Diocesan Synod: A Comparative Analysis of the 1917 and 1983 Codes of Canon Law," *Monitor Ecclesiasticus* 114 (1989): 560–572; Id., "Participation in the Synod," *Monitor Ecclesiasticus* 1116 (1991): 462–482; Gilles Routhier, "La synodalité de l'église locale," *Studia canonica* 26 (1992): 111–161.

9. For an overview of the function of the diocesan finance council, see Adrian Farrelly, "The Diocesan Finance Council: Functions and Duties according to the *Code of Canon Law*," *Studia canonica* 23 (1989): 149–166; John Myers, "The Diocesan Fiscal Officer and the Diocesan Finance Council," *CLSA Proceedings* 44 (1982): 181–188; Angelo Vizzari, "Il consiglio diocesano per gli affari economici: Constituzione, struttura, nomina," *Monitor Ecclesiasticus* 109 (1994): 269–290, 385–432; Heribert Schmitz, "Organe diozesaner Finanzverwaltung: Anmerkungen zu öffenstrittegen Fragen," *AkKR* 163 (1994): 121–145.

10. See Matthias Conrad, "De consilio pastorali paroeciali. Adnotationes in canonem 536 CIC/1983," *Periodica* 80 (1991): 45–91; William Dalton, "Parish Councils or Parish Pastoral Councils?" *Studia canonica* 22 (1988): 169–185; Agostino De Angelis, "I consigli per gli affari economici: statuti e indicazioni applicative," *Monitor Ecclesiasticus* 111 (1986): 57–68; P. Marcuzzi, "I consiglio pastorale parochiale," in *Ius in Vita et in Missione Ecclesiae*, 451–464; Roch Pagé, "The Parish Pastoral Council," *CLSA Proceedings* 43 (1981): 45–61; Jean-Claude Périsset, "La synodalité au niveau paroissal," *La Synodalité*, 2:805–814.

11. For a discussion of the particular problems involved in structuring these processes involving multiple parties, see John Beal, "Confining and Structuring Administrative Discretion: A Nuts and Bolts Approach," *CLSA Proceedings* 50 (1988): 98–104. See also Lawrence Susskind and Jeffrey Cruikshank, *Breaking the Impasse: Consensual Approaches to Resolving Public Policy Disputes* (New York: Basic Books, 1987).

12. Robert T. Kennedy, "Shared Responsibility in Ecclesial Decision-Making," *Studia canonica* 14 (1980): 9.

13. For a discussion of these other moments in the decision-making process, see Kennedy, 10–20.

14. Despite the infrequency of their occurrence, diocesan synods are considered the normal places for the bishop's exercise of his legislative authority. The most significant types of judicial trials are reserved to colleges of at least three judges (c. 1425, §§1–2). In the administrative arena, the code is suffused with requirements or at least recommendations that diocesan bishops consult with affected individuals or communities and with consultative bodies prior to acting. For example, see Thomas Green, "Consultation with Individuals or Groups Regarding Episcopal Discretion," in *Code, Community, Ministry*, Edward Pfnausch, ed. (Washington: CLSA, 1992).

15. Ruud Huysmans, "Le Code de Droit canonique fixe-t-il plutôt le fonctionnement exceptionnel que le fonctionnnment régulier du pouvoir dans l'Église catholique latine?" in *La Synodalité*, 93–95. A noteworthy exception to this tendency to impose as few fetters as possible on the discretion of ecclesiastical authorities is the law governing the administration of temporal goods where there is a long canonical tradition counseling consultative decision making.

16. Eugenio Corecco, "Theological Justifications of the Codification of the Latin Canon Law," in *The New Code of Canon Law. Fifth International Congress of Canon Law, Ottawa, 1984*, Michel Theriault and Jean Thorn, eds. (Ottawa: Faculty of Canon Law, Saint Paul University, 1986): 84–94.

17. Ibid., 91.

18. Eugenio Corecco, "Aspects of the Reception of Vatican II in the Code of Canon Law," in *The Reception of Vatican II*, Giuseppe Alberigo et al., eds. (Washington: The Catholic University of America Press, 1987): 281–282.

19. Analysis of the situation is further complicated by the equivocal use of the term "decree" in canon 145, §2, which stipulates that the obligations and rights of an office (its "job description") can be defined "in the decree of a competent authority by which it is at the same time constituted and conferred." In normal canonical usage, the decree establishing an office is a legislative decree whose issuance is reserved to the diocesan bishop, while the office is conferred by an executive decree, something that can, in principle, be issued by lower level authorities who enjoy only executive power of governance (c. 48).

20. Canons 526, §1 and 905, §2. See James Provost, "Temporary Replacements or New Forms of Ministry: Lay Persons with Pastoral Care of Parishes," In *Diversitate Unitas: Monsignor W. Onclin Chair 1997* (Leuven: Uitgeverij Peeters, 1997): 62–65.

21. For a practical guide to the new office of the lay person entrusted with the pastoral care of a parish and suggestions for how the office might be structured, see Barbara Anne Cusack and Therese Guerin Sullivan, *Pastoral Care in Parishes Without a Pastors: Applications of Canon 517, §2* (Washington: CLSA, 1995).

22. See Provost, "Temporary Replacements or New Forms of Ministry," 64–65.

23. For reflections on the experience of lay people entrusted with the pastoral care of parishes, see James Hoffman and John McRaith, "Adapting Parish Structures Within the Particular Church of the Twenty-First Century," *CLSA Proceedings* 56 (1994): 18–27; Antoine Finifini Mantenkadi, "L'expérience pastorale des responsables laïcs de paroisses (bakambi) au Zaïre: histoire et perspectives," *Studia canonica* 28 (1994): 155–166; Francis Messner, "Les laïcs chargés de la pastorale en R.F.A.," *L'Année canonique* 35 (1992): 77–86; Ad Van der Helm, *Un clergé parallèl?* (Strasbourg: CERDIC, 1993); and Ruth Wallace, *They Call Her Pastor: A New Role for Catholic Women* (Albany, N.Y.: State University of New York Press, 1992). For a discussion of the specifically canonical issues raised by this new institute see, Michael Böhnke, *Pastoral in Gemeinden ohne Pfarrer: Interpretation von c. 517 §2 CIC/1983*, Münsterische Kommentar zum Codex Iuris Canonici 12 (Essen: Ludgerus Verlag, 1994); Sharon Euart, RSM, "Parishes Without a Resident Pastor: Reflections on the Provisions and Conditions of Canon 517, §2 and its Implications," *The Jurist* 54 (1994): 369–408; Karl-Theodor Geringer, "Die deutschen Pfarrgemeinderäte als verfassungsrechtliches Problem," *Münchener Theologisches Zeitschrift 37* (1986): 42–57; Jean-Marie Huet, "Les nouvelles formes d'office curial (CIC, can 517)," *Nouvelle Revue Théologique 113* (1991): 47–74; John Renken, "Canonical Issues in the Pastoral Care of Parishes Without Priests," *The Jurist* 47 (1987): 506–521; Id., "Parishes Without a Resident Pastor: Comments on Canon 517, §2," *CLSA Proceedings* 50 (1988): 249–263; Heribert Schmitz, "'Gemeindeleitung' durch 'Nichtpfarrer-Priester' oder 'Nichtpriester-Pfarrer': Kanonistische Skizze zu den neuen Modell pfarrlicher Gemeindeleitung des c. 517, §2CIC," *AkKR* 161 (1992): 329–361; and Alexander A. Vadakumthala, "Lay Person as Caretaker of A Parish (A Juridical and Theological Study of Canon 517, 2)," *J.C.D. Dissertation* (Urbaniana University, Rome, 1992); Patrick Valdrini, "Charge pastorale et communautés hiérarchiques: Reflexions doctrinales pour l'application du canon 517,2" *L'Année canonique 37* (1995): 25–36.

24. Despite this rather modest job description, most commentators on the 1917 code held that the office of chancellor entailed the exercise of the power of jurisdiction at least insofar as he could grant or deny access to the diocesan archives. See the discussion of this issue in John Prince, "The Diocesan Chancellor: An Historical Synopsis and Commentary," *Canon Law Studies* 167 (Washington: The Catholic University of America, 1942): 45–47. Since the job description for the office of the chancellor is the same in the 1983 code as it was in the 1917 code, one must presume that the office continues to entail a jurisdictional dimension. Thus, the opening of this office to lay people in the revised code may be seen as yet another exception within the code itself to the stricture of canon 274, §1, which restricts access to offices entailing the power of governance to clergy.

25. James Provost, "Diocesan Administration: Reflections on Recent Developments," *The Jurist* 41 (1981): 81–104.

26. Prior to the promulgation of the 1983 code, some had argued that lay judges in ecclesiastical tribunals did not really exercise jurisdiction because in marriage cases—the only cases in which they were permitted to function at that time—they did not impose obligations but merely declared juridic facts. See Klaus Lüdicke, "Laien als kirchlicher Richter. Über den Inhalt des kirchlichen Richteramtes," *ÖAKR* 28 (1977): 332–352 and Roch Pagé, "Juges laïcs et exercise de pouvoir judiciaire," in *Unico Ecclesiae Servitio: Canonical Studies Presented to Germain Lesage, O.M.I.*, Michel Thériault and Jean Thorn, eds. (Ottawa: Saint Paul University, 1991): 197–212. The promulgation of the 1983 code, which allows the use

of lay judges to form a college in any type of case, has rendered the issue moot. Others have claimed and continue to claim that it is not the lay judge but the college of judges that exercises power of governance. See Wilhelm Bertrams, "Communio, communitas, societas in Lege Fundamentali Ecclesiae," *Periodica* 61 (1972): 595. However, most canonists who oppose the granting of jurisdiction to lay people agree with Mörsdorf that such ingenious attempts to avoid the obvious conclusion that lay judges do indeed exercise jurisdiction is "a game of hide and seek that does not take the significance of the norm seriously." See Klaus Mörsdorf, "Die Weihesakrament in seiner Tragweite für den verfassungsrechtlichen Aufbau der Kirche," *Schriften zum kanonischen Recht,* Winfried Aymans et al., eds. (Paderborn: Ferdinand Schöningh, 1989): 238. They counsel that canon 1421, §2 is bad law and should be abrogated or at least not implemented.

27. Unlike the 1917 code, the revised code makes clear that the administration of the Church's temporal goods is a function of the power of governance. See c. 1273: "By virtue of his primacy in governance the Roman Pontiff is the supreme administrator and steward of all ecclesiastical goods." See also c. 1290.

28. For an overview of the canonical discussion of the possibility of granting lay people a share in the power of governance through delegation, see Beatrix Laukemper-Isermann, *Zur Mitarbeit von Laien in der bischöflichen Verwaltung: Rechtliche Möglichkeiten der Anwendung des can. 129, §2 CIC,* Münsterische Kommentar zum Codez Iuris Canonici 16 (Essen: Ludgerus Verlag, 1996): 56–61.

29. Proponents of this position include Wilhelm Bertrams and the late Klaus Mörsdorf as well as most of their disciples. For a discussion of the approaches of these schools to the question of exercise of power of governance by lay people, see Beal, "State of the Question," 18–35.

30. Protagonists of this position include Jean Beyer and Gianfranco Ghirlanda of the Pontifical Gregorian University and, from a somewhat different perspective, numerous canonists associated with the University of Navarre and, more recently, the Ateneo Romano della Santa Croce. See Beal, "State of the Question," 35–52.

31. Edward Kilmartin, "Lay Participation in the Apostolate of the Hierarchy," *The Jurist* 41 (1981): 352–353.

32. The critical role of the distinction between the common and the ministerial priesthoods for these theories makes it difficult for them to account for the fact that deacons are habiles for the power of governance even though, as *Lumen Gentium* no. 29 noted, they are ordained "non ad sacerdotium, sed ad ministerium."

33. Klaus Mörsdorf, "Das eine Volk Gottes und der Teilhabe der Laien in der Sendung des Kirches," in *Ecclesia et Ius: Festgabe für Audomar Scheuermann zum 60. Geburtstag,* K. Siepen et al., eds. (Munich: Ferdinand Schöningh, 1968): 103.

34. For an overview of the deliberations of the Code Commission on this issue, see Beal, "State of the Question," 52–66; Emilio Malumbres, "Los laicos y la potesdad de regimen en los trabajos de reforma codicial: una cuestion convertida," *Ius Canonicum* 26 (1986): 563–625; and Thomas Amann, *Laien als Träger von Leitungsgewalt? Eine Untersuchung*

aufgrund des Codex Iuris Canonici, Münchener Theologische Studien, Kanonistische Abteilung, 50. Band (St. Ottilien, EOS Verlag, 1996), 31–64.

35. For the views of those who believe lay people cannot be given a share in the power of governance, see David-Maria Jaeger, "The Relationship of Holy Orders and the Power of Governance According to the Revised *Code of Canon Law* or: Are the Laity Capable of the Power of Governance?" *Canon Law Society of Great Britain and Ireland Newsletter* no. 62 (September 1984): 20–38; Winfried Aymans, *Lehrbuch des kanonisches Recht aufgrund des Codex Iuris Canonici* (Paderborn: Ferdinand Schöningh): 1: 385–424; and Amann, 85–158. For the views of those who believe lay people can be given a share in the power of governance, see Jean Beyer, "Iudex laicus vir et mulier," *Periodica* 75 (1986): 29–60; Gianfranco Ghirlanda, "De natura, origine et exercitio potestatis regiminis iuxta novum Codicem," *Periodica* 74 (1985): 109–164; and Francisco Urrutia, "Delegation of the Executive Power of Governance," *Studia canonica* 19 (1985): 338–355. See also Javier Hervada, *Elementos de Derecho Constitucional Canonico* (Pamplona: EUNSA, 1987): 235–250.

36. Jaeger, 27.

37. See cc. 124, §1; 1057,§1; 1674, and perhaps 241, §1. See Xaverius Ochoa, *Index verborum ac locutionum Codicis Iuris Canonici* (Vatican City: Libreria Editrice Lateranense, 1984): 210. However, all of these canons except one merely distinguish those who are *habiles* in general from those who are *inhabiles* in general. They do not identify classes of persons who are (or are not) *habiles.* Thus, canon 1057, §1 simply states that "marriage is brought about through the consent . . . between persons who are *iure habiles.*" One must look elsewhere for the conditions or qualities required to render these persons *habiles* or *inhabiles.* Only canon 1674, which recognizes the spouses and, in some cases, the promoter of justice as *habiles* to impugn the validity of a marriage, clearly identifies the *habiles* and implicitly renders all others *inhabiles.*

38. See cc. 229, §3; 228, §§1–2; 254, §2. See Ochoa, *Index verborum,* 210.

39. Beyer, "Iudex laicus," 40–41.

40. "Opera Consultorum in parandis canonum schematibus," *Communicationes* 3 (1971): 187.

41. Proponents of this view are Jaeger, 27 and Aymans, 400.

42. For the use of *cooperari,* see cc. 208; 328, 529, §2; 625, §4; 759; and 796,§2. For the use of *cooperator,* see cc. 245, §2; 545, §1; 651, §2; 652, §1; and 757. For the use *cooperatio,* see 275, §1; 296; 369; 434; 680; 708; 713, §2; 782, §1; 791; 820; 1096, §1; 1274, §4. See Ochoa, *Index verborum,* 115.

43. "Canon 1400, §2: Controversies from an Act of Administrative Power," in *Roman Replies and CLSA Advisory Opinions 1991,* Kevin Vann and Lynn Jarrell, eds. (Washington: CLSA, 1991), 36. The precedential value of such a private reply is, of course, limited.

44. Canon 969, §1 explicitly stipulates that "only the local ordinary is competent to confer" on presbyters the faculty to hear confessions. For an analysis of other areas where the nature of the matter may restrict a diocesan bishops capacity to delegate power of governance to lay people, see Laukemper-Isermann, 74–87.

45. Felix Cappello, *Summa Iuris Canonici* (Rome: Apud Aedes Pontificiae Universitatis Gregorianae, 1962), 2:231: "Ordinarius etiam personae non capaci iurisdictionis ecclesiasticae, e.g., Antistitae sive Superiorissae, permittere potest modo generali aut particulari designationum sacerdotum quos ipse Ordinarius, posita ista conditione, delegare intendit ad confessiones audiendas. Ita ex. gr. statuere potest: omnes sacerdotes qui ad Sacrum faciendum in sacello religiosiarum admittantur, habiles reddo ad confessiones ibi excipiendas. In casu iurisdictio *expresse* concessa intelligitur ad normam can. 879, §1 [1917 CIC]." However, the institute of designation is not applicable to the special delegation of priests or deacons to witness marriages since canon 1111, §2 requires that "to be valid the delegation of the faculty to assist at marriages must be given expressly to specified persons; if it is a question of special delegation, it is to be granted for a specific marriage." See Pontificia Commissio Codici Iuris Canonici Interpretendo, Responsa ad dubium, May 20, 1923: *AAS* 16 (1923): 115 and John Beal, "Canon 1111, §2: Delegation for Marriage by Designation," in *Roman Replies and CLSA Advisory Opinions 1996*, Kevin Vann and James Donlon, eds. (Washington: CLSA, 1996), 100–101.

46. "Canon 1400, §2: Controversies from an Act of Administrative Power," 37–38.

47. Congar, *Lay People in the Church*, 268–269.

48. Cyprian, Ep. xiv, 4.

Magisterial Teaching
BY FRANCIS CARDINAL GEORGE, OMI, PH.D.

This paper identifies those expressions of magisterial teaching since Vatican II that speak to the development of ministry. A preliminary note on the council's central insight that the Church is a communion comments that it is a communion that "allows for the simultaneous expression of sacramental equality and hierarchical order." Within the communion of the faithful, the episcopacy and ordained priesthood make visible the headship of Christ. It is necessary to distinguish between ecclesial lay ministry and the apostolic work to which baptism calls every Christian. The note concludes "if the relationships rooted in sacramental communion are respected, ministerial functions sort themselves out."

The synopsis of relevant magisterial documents includes Lumen Gentium; Apostolicam Actuositatem; *the* Final Report *on the* Extraordinary Synod on the Laity; Christifideles Laici; Redemptoris Missio; *the May 1992 letter from the Congregation for the Doctrine of the Faith on "Some Aspects of the Church Understood as Communion"; a papal address to the participants in the (April 1994) Symposium on the Participation of the Laity in the Priestly Ministry; six "marginal references"; and the National Conference of Catholic Bishops' document* Called and Gifted.

Introduction

The charge given to me is to identify those expressions of magisterial teaching since Vatican II that speak to the development of lay ministry. The documents are presented so that, as much as possible, they can inform the discussion by speaking for themselves. A preliminary interpretive note, however, can remind us that the Second Vatican Council's central insight was the rediscovery of the intrinsic, sacramental relationship between the mystery of Christ and the Church. "The Church, in Christ, is in the nature of sacrament—a sign and instrument, that is, of communion with God and of unity among all men."[1]

Because the Church is "a communion of life, love, and truth," the Church understands itself to be the "instrument for the salvation of all; as the light of the world and the salt of the earth it is sent forth into the whole world."[2] All of the Vatican documents, most particularly *Lumen Gentium's* considerable articulation of the Church's nature, mission, and ministries, assumed and built upon this dynamic of universal communion.

In the years since the council, subsequent magisterial teaching has led to a deeper understanding of communion and consequently of the ministry that serves ecclesial communion. Twenty years after the close of Vatican II, John Paul II called an Extraordinary Synod of Bishops to assess and to reaffirm the council. The synodal reflection of those assembled bishops furthered Vatican II's ecclesiology of communion by affirming that "communion is the central and fundamental idea of the Council's documents."[3] The synod noted that "the structures and relations within the Church must express this communion."[4]

How did the synod fathers understand communion? Fundamentally, they perceived communion as relationship with God through Jesus Christ realized through the power of the Holy Spirit and made visible sacramentally in the Church. Communion, initiated in baptism, draws most powerfully upon the eucharist as "the source and the culmination of the whole Christian life."[5] The synod stressed that "the communion of the eucharistic body of Christ signifies and produces, that is, builds up, the intimate communion of all the faithful in the body of Christ which is the Church."[6] For this reason, declared the bishops, "the ecclesiology of communion cannot be reduced to purely organizational questions or to problems which simply relate to powers."[7]

The synodal appreciation of communion, with its profound eucharistic dependence, was echoed seven years later by the Congregation for the Doctrine of the Faith in its letter to the bishops of the Catholic Church, *Some Aspects of the Church Understood as Communion.* "Ecclesial communion, into which each individual is introduced by faith and by baptism," wrote the congregation, "has its root and center in the Holy Eucharist."[8] The congregation's letter stressed that "the Eucharist is the creative force and source of communion among the members of the

Church, precisely because it unites each one of them with Christ Himself."[9]

What does the Church express when it speaks of communion? At its core, communion articulates the mysterious union of each human being with the blessed Trinity through Jesus Christ and in the Church. Beyond any human expression, ecclesial communion points to the very mystery of the triune God. At the heart of faith is the mystery of the Trinity, God's existence in relationship.[10] The Church is a mystery of communion because it arises from and is centered in the mystery of God.

Divine revelation teaches that God is Father, Son, and Spirit—a communion of persons. Trinitarian relatedness defines humanity in general and the Church in particular. Made in the image of the relational God, members of the human family are called not to self-interest but to love of the other—of God and neighbor. Through ecclesial communion, through relationship with God and the Church, human beings find fulfilled their purpose as created and redeemed beings.

Jesus, in communion with his Father and the Spirit through their divine nature shared in one substance, experiences communion with men and women through human nature shared by many substances. Participant in trinitarian communion, Jesus Christ brings men and women into relationship with God through mediating God's life to them. As the unifying possession of the baptized, Christ creates their ecclesial communion, in which the divine life of grace is made visible or that it can be shared.

Christ, the center of communion, joins the baptized together through the gift of the Spirit; through faith, sacraments and ecclesiastical structure (LG 13, 14, 15; OE 4, 30; UR 3e) he relates the Church to the Father in a single visible communion and a common vocation. Called to proclaim the communion it realizes, the Church's vocation is to be a living conduit of the Trinity. The Church exists to make God's redemptive love accessible through the communion of its life. Just as Christ came to do the work of the Father, the Church exists to continue Christ's mission "that they might be one" (Jn 17:11).

Since God's own relational communion contains both unity and distinction (CCC, no. 255), ecclesial communion also expresses unity and diversity. The Church is the sign and the instrument of unity among diverse peoples and conditions.[11] Within communion, the Church's hierarchy maintains unity and fosters diversity so as to ensure its mission. As communion, the Church cannot be separated from its mission. The diversity present in the complementarity of ecclesial vocations, charisms, ministries, and responsibilities exists within a unity of being and of oneness of mission. That mission calls all the baptized to foster communion and to proclaim the Gospel. The communion of the Church involves "a most solid unity and, on the other hand, a plurality and diversification which do not obstruct unity, but rather confer upon it the character of communion."[12]

Regrettably, an ecclesiology of communion is sometimes presented as an alternative to ecclesial hierarchy. No such opposition exists. The Church is an organic whole, not a collection of extrinsically related individuals. In fact, the theology of communion allows for the simultaneous expression of baptismal equality and hierarchical order. The Church's authority is not the authority of secular power but the authority of truth emanating from God, before whom all the baptized possess equal dignity (LG, no. 32).

Ministry expresses ecclesial authority in two forms. First is the authority of all the baptized who, as members of Christ's body, share the priestly, prophetic, and kingly office of Christ (LG, no. 31). There is also the authority of those called to ordination—an authority of service to the baptized. Within a proper appreciation of communion, ecclesial authority is seen as a center of relationships among members of the same body— as the head is such a center in a physical body.

Authority is inherent to communion, because it makes visible the Church's unity in Christ. The authority of the Church reflects a divine dynamic communicated through ecclesial communion. Christianity is essentially life in perpetual self-transcendence not only toward and into God in Christ but also toward and into Christ in the communion of the Church.

The communion that gives definition to the people of God is therefore a sacramental communion of a hierarchical order. As *Lumen Gentium's nota praevia explicativa* of November 16, 1964 stated, "Communion is a concept held in high honor in the ancient Church. By it is meant not some vague sentiment but an organic reality that calls for juridical expression and yet at the same time is ensouled by love."

A solid appreciation of the ecclesiology of communion is essential to understanding the post-Vatican II development of lay ministry. All ministry renews the life of the Church and enables the Church to transform the world. The Church cannot be dissociated from the ministries that manifest its communion—especially the episcopate. Succeeding to the apostolic college, the episcopate is the ministry of communion that maintains the unity of the *koinonia*. Episcopal consecration confers "together with the office of sanctifying, the duty of teaching and ruling which . . . can be exercised only in hierarchical communion with the head and members of the college" (LG, no. 21). The episcopal college makes universal ecclesial communion visible, much as each of the baptized makes visible the Church in the world and as the ordained priesthood makes visible the relationship between Christ and his bride. Within the communion of the faithful, the episcopacy and the ordained priesthood make the headship of Christ visible.

Vatican II taught clearly that the lay faithful are responsible for the mission of the Church. Participation in the Church's mission to the world is rooted in baptism. The conciliar documents speak of the dignity of all the baptized and stress their primary mission to transform the world. But the documents also offer a renewed understanding of lay participation within the Church. *Apostolicam Actuositatem* affirmed that the lay faithful have an "active part of their own in the life and action of the Church. Their action within the Church communities is so necessary that without it the apostolate of the pastors will frequently be unable to obtain its full effect."[13]

Lay ministry serves ecclesial communion through teaching, liturgical ministry, administration, pastoral care, and the outreach of charity and justice—all in the name of Christ and his Church. Lay ministry, however, does not include automatically all the efforts of the baptized. There is a necessary distinction between ecclesial lay ministry and the apostolic work every Christian is called to do by reason of baptism.

Ministry originates with the Holy Spirit distributing gifts with communion. In *Christifideles Laici,* the pope emphasized that lay ministries are gifts of the Spirit, given for building up the Body of Christ. The Holy Spirit "lavishes diverse hierarchical and charismatic gifts on all the baptized, calling them to be, each in an individual way, active and co-responsible."[14] However, lay ministry arises not only out of personal charism but more fundamentally out of the relationship to Christ sacramentally mediated by baptism and confirmation (CFL, no. 20).

Any ministry must be identified and delegated subsequently by the ordained pastors according to the nature of the ministry and an individual's state within the communion. Ministry does not emanate from scarcity, right, or even personal ability. As Paul VI noted in *Evangelii Nuntiandi,* the laity can be called to "work with their pastors in the service of the ecclesial community, for its growth and life, by exercising a great variety of gifts and ministries according to the grace and charisms which the Lord is pleased to give them."[15]

But because all ministry is a participation in the ministry of Jesus Christ, the exercise of those ministries must reflect the relationships established within Christ's Church. The ministries of the lay faithful ought to be in conformity to their specific vocation, which is different from that of the ordained ministry (CFL, no. 23). As the *Decree on the Church's Missionary Activity* stated, "The Church is not truly established and does not fully live, nor is it a perfect sign of Christ unless there is a genuine laity existing and working alongside the hierarchy" (AG, no. 21). If the relationships rooted in sacramental communion are respected, ministerial functions sort themselves out. The drawing of distinctions is done as much to safeguard lay initiative as it is to make clear the essential difference between the priesthood of the baptized and that of the ordained.

Synopsis of Relevant Magisterial Documents

The Dogmatic Constitution on the Church—*Lumen Gentium*
November 21, 1964

In the fourth chapter of *Lumen Gentium*, the Second Vatican Council addressed the nature and responsibility of the laity understood as "all the faithful except those in Holy Orders or in a religious state" (LG, no. 31). The fathers stressed that all the baptized faithful "in their own way share the priestly, prophetic and kingly office of Christ" (LG, no. 31). The laity are charged with carrying on the mission of the Church in the world. It is the world that provides the particular context of the lay mission.

Secularity contextualizes their identity and defines their vocation. By reason of lay people's secular character, they are to seek the kingdom of God by engaging in temporal affairs and directing them according to God's will (LG, no. 31). Living out their baptismal identity and ecclesial mission in the world, the laity engage in every work and business, in all the ordinary circumstances of social and family life.

It is in the particular area of public witness that the laity most completely exercise their vocation. The laity become powerful heralds of the faith if they unhesitatingly profess their life in Christ. This living evangelization—the proclamation of Christ by word and life—acquires a peculiar efficacy when accomplished in the ordinary circumstances of the world (LG, no. 35). The laity play a principal role not only in the evangelization of the world but in reforming the conditions, cultures, and institutions of the world so that these are in greater harmony with the Gospel.

Acknowledging that not all members of the Church have the same gifts or responsibilities, the council fathers nonetheless insisted on the common dignity and the shared vocation to holiness of all the baptized. Called to holiness, the laity share in the salvific mission of the Church in a way distinct from those in sacred orders. The distinction between the ordained and lay ministries, however, should elicit cooperation rather than competition (LG, no. 32). The council specifically noted that the laity can be called into active ecclesial service by their pastors;

the laity enjoy "the capacity of being appointed by the hierarchy to some ecclesiastical offices with a view to a spiritual end" (LG, no. 33).

Thus, the knowledge and competency of the laity is to be brought to bear not only on the institutions of the world but also within the life of the Church itself (LG, no. 37). Pastors should "recognize and promote the dignity and responsibility of the laity in the Church. They should willingly use their prudent advice and confidently assign duties to them in the service of the Church, leaving them freedom and scope for acting. Indeed, they should give them the courage to undertake works on their own initiative" (LG, no. 37).

The call to ecclesial ministry first set forth in *Lumen Gentium* was later echoed in *Evangelii Nuntiandi* in its acknowledgment that "the laity can also feel themselves called, or be called, to work with their pastors in the service of the ecclesial community, for its growth and life, by exercising a great variety of gifts and ministries according to the grace and charisms which the Lord is pleased to give them." These ecclesial ministries are "capable of renewing and strengthening the evangelizing vigour of the Church" (EN, no. 53).

Decree on the Apostolate of the Laity—*Apostolicam Actuositatem* November 18, 1965

Building on the foundation of *Lumen Gentium* the fathers, near the conclusion of the council, issued their decree on the *Apostolate of the Laity*. Recognizing the indispensable role of the laity in the mission of the Church, the council noted that "the Christian vocation is, of its nature, a vocation to the apostolate as well." (AA, no. 2) By *apostolate*, the fathers meant every activity of the Church. As a consequence of the relationship established by baptism, the lay faithful share Christ's priestly, prophetical, and kingly office, although they are called to exercise this office primarily in the temporal order.

The lay apostolate arises from the relationship with Christ in baptism and confirmation, which brings the laity into ecclesial communion. Within this dynamic of mutual relationships, the special gifts and charisms of the lay faithful are to be used in service. The laity are to exercise their apostolate, therefore, both in the world in general and, in a more particular manner, in the Church.

The Church as the context for the lay apostolate transforms lay activity into ministry. Within the general life of the Church, specific expressions of the lay apostolate were noted. These included participation in liturgical life, apostolic works, evangelization, catechetical instruction, care of souls, and the administration of the goods of the Church. The parish is to be the primary arena for these efforts.

The fields of the lay apostolate, however, far exceed ecclesial confines. The renewal of the world is the "distinctive task" of the laity (AA, no. 7). The laity have a particular opportunity for evangelization. By word, action, and their lives, they can witness to Christ. The family, youth, and secular communities at the local, national, and international levels are also vital fields of action. Not only can the laity exercise their apostolic activity at various levels but they also can act singly or in various associations.

Individuals can exercise extraordinary service in those circumstances where the life of the Church is hampered or threatened. In such circumstances, "the laity take over as far as possible the work of priests, jeopardizing their own freedom and sometimes their lives; they teach Christian doctrine to those around them, train them in a religious way of life and in Catholic attitudes, encourage them to receive the sacraments frequently and to cultivate piety" (AA, no. 17).

For lay persons serving the Church, adequate formation is indispensable. Since the laity participate in the Church's mission in ways appropriate to their character, their training must also be proper to their service and state. Different types of apostolate require their own method of training. These include
   a. the apostolate of evangelization and sanctification: the laity are to be specially trained for engaging in dialogue with others;
   b. the Christian renewal of the temporal order: the laity are to be instructed in the true meaning and value of temporal goods; and
   c. witness to Christ in redeeming grace: works of charity and mercy are the laity's testimony to the power of God's love.

Wherever the lay apostolate is exercised, it is always incorporated into the life of the Church "according to a right system of relationships" (AA, no. 23). The council fathers were careful to admonish the "need for mutual esteem among all the forms of the apostolate . . . with due respect for the proper character of each" (AA, no. 23). The hierarchy is directed to foster, to support, and to direct properly the apostolate of the laity. Lay ministerial undertakings must be with the consent of the lawful ecclesiastical authority (AA, no. 24).

The council recognized a variety of forms of lay apostolate, even noting that for pastoral reasons "the hierarchy joins some particular form of it more closely with its own apostolic function, leaving intact the proper nature and distinctiveness of each apostolate, and not depriving the laity of the opportunity of acting on their own accord" (AA, no. 24). It is of particular note that the decree recognizes the importance of entrusting to the laity "certain functions which are more closely connected with pastoral duties, such as the teaching of Christian doctrine, certain liturgical actions, in the care of souls" (AA, no. 24).

Extraordinary Synod of Bishops—*Final Report*
December 8, 1985

Twenty years after the close of the Second Vatican Council, an extraordinary session of the Synod of Bishops was called by John Paul II to "celebrate, verify, and promote the Council." In considering coresponsibility in the Church since Vatican II, the bishops specifically noted "a new style of collaboration" between the laity and clerics. They praised the "spirit of willingness" evidenced in the post-conciliar period of lay people who have generously put themselves at the service of the Church (FR, 449). This participation in the life of the Church was contextualized by a sense of ecclesial communion which involves mutually interdependent levels of participation and coresponsibility.

The Extraordinary Synod of Bishops represented a subtle shift in the ecclesiology, not in outright contradictions or explicit qualifications but in emphasis. Like a prism turned ever so slightly, the *Final Report* suggests not so much new colors but different hues. In perhaps the clearest magisterial reflection on the council, the synod stated that "the ecclesiology of communion is the central and fundamental idea of the Council documents" (FR, 448).

Communion allows for the proper recognition of lay participation in the Church. This ecclesiological shift appears particularly in reference to the synod's treatment of the Church as communion. The *Final Report* states that "the ecclesiology of communion is a central and fundamental idea in the documents of the council." The synod fathers saw communion as "the foundation for order in the Church, and especially for a correct relationship between unity and pluriformity" (FR, 448).

What did the bishops mean by communion? The *Final Report* defines it as a manner of "communion with God through Jesus Christ in the Holy Spirit. This communion exists through the Word of God and the sacraments" (FR, 448). Communion is a relationship that arises through the sharing of God's gifts in the Church.

A second aspect of communion is also mentioned: that of institutional unity and authority. The synod did not see an explicit tension between participation and authority within the ecclesiology of communion. In fact, in addressing certain key ecclesiological concepts, this tension does not contradict Vatican II but seems to focus on its teaching. Communion emerged as the means of balancing a variety of ecclesiological elements.

Communion is presented as a corrective to a misunderstanding that the synod felt had developed since Vatican II. As the *Final Report* stated ". . . a partial reading of the council has caused a one-sided presentation of the Church as a merely institutional structure, deprived of its mystery" (FR, 445). The council responded by warning against substituting "for the false, one-sided, merely hierarchical notion of the Church, just a new one-sided sociological concept" (FR). An ecclesiology of communion arising from the mystery of the Trinity allows for adjustment without over-correction.

While the Final Report noted various conciliar descriptions of the Church, the synod saw the notion of communion as the most compelling.

Significantly, John Paul II highlighted this ecclesiological shift on December 7, when he noted that what the synod had done was to reveal more fully "the nature of the Church so far as it is a mystery and communion."

Communion also provided the basis for addressing the potentially troublesome issue of collegiality. "The ecclesiology of communion provides a sacramental foundation for collegiality," stated the *Final Report.* Collegiality is not to be understood just in a juridic sense, but also as a "collegial spirit." Communion provided the theological basis for other "signs and instruments" of the collegial spirit: the Synod of Bishops, bishops' conferences, etc. An ecclesiology of communion allows for participation and discipline while maintaining the sacramental nature of the Church rooted in the mystery of the Trinity.

Post-Synodal Apostolic Exhortation on the Vocation and the Mission of the Lay Faithful in the Church and in the World—*Christifideles Laici*
December 30, 1988

The topic for the 1987 Synod of Bishops was "Vocation and Mission in the Church and in the World Twenty Years after the Second Vatican Council." The month-long deliberation of bishops from around the world provided the basis for John Paul II's post-synodal apostolic exhortation, *Christifideles Laici.* Arising as it did out of a powerful experience of ecclesial communion, it is a landmark reflection on the nature and apostolate of the lay faithful. In it the pope eloquently affirms the dignity and mission of the laity as "laborers in the vineyard."

Stressing the spirit of collaboration, the pope employs the concept of communion to contextualize the lay vocation. Ecclesial communion is more precisely likened to an "organic" communion characterized by a diversity and a complementarity of vocations and states in life, of ministries, of charisms and of responsibilities. Because of this diversity and complementarity, every member of the lay faithful is seen in relation to the whole body and offers a totally unique contribution on behalf of the whole body (CL, no. 20).

The nature of ecclesial lay ministry is addressed within the context of the lay character and the mystery of ecclesial communion. The document understands both of these realities in relationship to each other. "Only from inside the Church's mystery of communion is the 'identity' of the lay faithful made known" (CL, no. 8). The Holy Father presents lay identity as rooted in baptism, wherein the laity are constituted as members of the Church and sharers in the priestly, prophetic and kingly office of Christ (CL, no. 9).

The life of the lay faithful is directed to "a knowledge of the radical newness of the Christian life that comes from baptism." The regeneration received in baptism creates a real but mystical incorporation into Christ and joins the baptized together. Through the outpouring of the Holy Spirit received in baptism and confirmation, the lay faithful, in communion with Christ and one another share in the one mission of Christ (CL, no. 12).

Through the entire People of God, the mission of Christ—priest, prophet, king—continues in the Church. The lay faithful share in Christ's priestly mission in that, united to him, they offer themselves through their daily activities in general, and through the eucharist in particular. Participating in Christ's prophetic mission, they proclaim the Gospel in word and deed, allowing the power of the Gospel to shine in them, their activities, and their relationships. Sharing in the kingly mission, they spread the kingdom by combating in themselves and in the world the power of sin (CFL, no. 14). Because lay participation in the threefold mission is derived from ecclesial communion, that mission must be lived and realized in communion (CL, no. 14).

The newness of life received in baptism is the basis for the common dignity of the faithful. "But among the lay faithful this one baptismal dignity takes on a manner in life which sets a person apart, without, however, bringing about a separation from the ministerial priesthood or from men and women religious" (CL, no. 15). This secular character is properly and particularly that of the lay faithful (CL, no. 15).

The dignity conferred in baptism, to be actualized in the secular order, is directed toward the vocation to holiness. Holiness is the fundamental vocation of the baptized. It is not a simple moral exhortation but an undeniable requirement arising from communion. The Church is the choice vine, whose branches live and grow with the same hold and life-giving energies that come from Christ (CL, no. 16). For the lay faithful, holiness, rooted in baptism and renewed in eucharist, expresses itself in the life of the Church and participation in earthly activities. Holiness is "intimately connected to mission and to the responsibility entrusted to the lay faithful in the Church and in the world" (CL, no. 17).

Holiness would not be possible without the dignity conferred in baptism. The dignity of the Christian flows from the sacramentally mediated relationship established with Christ in the Church. Because the baptized are one with Christ and consequently with each other, Christians possess an intrinsic dignity and equality. This dignity fosters the communion that is the hidden force of the Church's mission (CL, no. 17). Christians no longer belong to themselves but are the Lord's. "I am the vine, you are the branches."

The pope is careful to point out that communion is not a recent invention of the Church. Rather, it finds its source in Sacred Scripture and was a concept held in great honor in the early Church and in the Oriental Churches (CL, no. 19). The pope acknowledged, however, that the Second Vatican Council provoked a clearer understanding of communion. The council provided a renewed sense of union with God, with the sacramental life of the Church as the starting point. Baptism is the door and the foundation, but the eucharist maintains the intimate bond of communion—as its source and summit.

Sacramental communion leads to a double, life-giving participation: "the incorporation of Christians into the life of Christ; and the communication of that life of charity to the entire body of the Faithful, in this world and in the next, through union with Christ and in Christ, and union among Christians, in the Church" (CL, no. 19). Communion is central to salvation. Therefore, communion "cannot be interpreted in a sufficient way if it is understood as simply a sociological or a psychological reality" (CL, no. 19).

The pope likened ecclesial communion to an "organic" bond characterized by diversity and complementarity. One and the same Spirit is always the dynamic principle of diversity and unity. Every member of the lay faithful is seen in relation to the whole body and offers a unique contribution to the whole body (CL, no. 20). Ecclesial communion is a gift of the Holy Spirit, who guides the Church and unifies it in communion. The Spirit bestows upon the Church varied hierarchical and charismatic gifts, inviting people to assume different ministries and forms of service. What distinguishes persons is capacity for service within the communion. The charisms, the ministries, the different forms of service exercised by the lay faithful only exist in and for communion (CL, no. 20).

Yet communion needs a proper hierarchy to facilitate ministerial service. The ordained ministries are in a primary position. The sacrament of orders conveys the authority to serve the Church in persona *Christi Capitis*. Ordained ministers realize the priesthood of Jesus Christ in a manner different—not simply in degree but in essence—from that of the lay faithful through baptism and confirmation. But as the Second Vatican Council noted, it must never be forgotten that the ministerial priesthood has the royal priesthood of all the faithful as its aim and is ordered to it. The pope strongly urged pastors to "acknowledge and foster the ministries, the offices and roles of the lay faithful that find their foundation in the Sacraments of Baptism and Confirmation" (CL, no. 23).

When necessity and expediency require, wrote the pope, the pastors can entrust to the lay faithful certain offices connected to their pastoral ministry. He cautioned, however, that the exercise of such tasks does not make pastors of the lay faithful. A person is not a pastor simply in performing a task but through a relationship borne of sacramental ordination.

Lay pastoral ministry takes its legitimacy formally and immediately from the official deputation given by the pastors. An indiscriminate use of "ministry" confuses both the common priesthood and the ministerial priesthood. Similarly, the pope warned that the failure to observe ecclesiastical laws and norms tends toward a "clericalization" of the lay faithful and risks creating an ecclesial structure parallel to that of orders (CL, no. 23).

To avoid this danger, the synod fathers had called for a greater clarity in expressing both "the unity of the Church's mission in which all the baptized participate, and the substantial diversity of the ministry of Pastors which is rooted in the Sacrament of Orders, all the while respecting the other ministers, offices and roles in the Church, which are rooted in the Sacraments of Baptism and Confirmation" (CL, no. 23).

To accomplish that goal, the pope directed that, in conferring various ministries, offices, and roles, maximum care be exercised to institute ministries on the basis of baptism. The pope also cautioned pastors against an abusive recourse to a "situation of emergency that objectively does not exist." Lay ministry ought to be exercised in conformity to the lay vocation, which is a vocation different from that of the ordained ministry.

The bestowal of ministries should not be confused with the imparting of charisms. The Holy Spirit enriches the Church with particular charisms. Charisms are graces that directly or indirectly foster the ecclesial community. The discernment of charisms, however, is always necessary. Therefore, no charism dispenses a person from submission to the pastors of the Church (CL, no. 24).

The lay faithful participate in the life of the Church not only in exercising ministries but also in living their individual charisms. Such participation finds it most immediate forum in the parish. The parish is the place where the very "mystery" of the Church is present and at work. Because it is a community constituted by ordained ministers and other Christians, it is a community properly suited for celebrating the eucharist.

The full participation of the lay faithful in parish life is so necessary that without it the apostolate of the pastors would be unable to achieve its full effectiveness. Because of each member's unique and irrepeatable character, each individual is placed at the service of the growth of the parish while, at the same time, participating in and benefitting from the richness of the Church particular and universal.

John Paul II made specific reference to the forms of lay participation in the Church. He acknowledged both individual and group service. Each member of the lay faithful is a member of the Church entrusted with a unique task. Regardless of whether it is exercised individually or collectively, all lay persons are called to contribute to spreading the Gospel (CL, no. 28).

Communion, already present in the activities of the individual, finds its specific expression in the lay faithful's working together in groups. Such lay groups have received a special stimulus resulting in the birth and the spread of a multiplicity of group forms: associations, groups, communities, and movements. Lay groups show themselves to be very diverse. However, all come together in their common purpose, that is, the responsible participation of all of them in the Church's mission of spreading the Gospel of Christ.

In an increasingly secularized world, various forms of the lay apostolate can foster Christian life and fidelity. Beyond mere pragmatism, however, the profound justification for the lay faithful working together in groups is an ecclesiology of communion as the Second Vatican Council acknowledged in referring to the group apostolate as "a sign of communion and of unity of the Church of Christ" (AA, no. 18).

Encyclical on Missionary Activity—*Redemptoris Missio*
December 7, 1990
In his encyclical addressing the Church's missionary activity, *Redemptoris Missio*, John Paul II defined the frontiers of missionary activity as extending not only to all nations but to a reevangelization of traditionally Christian areas. In reviewing the Church's missionary imperative, the pope wrote at length about the laity as missionaries.

Referring to his earlier encyclical *Christifideles Laici*, wherein he had clearly noted the importance of lay missionary activity, John Paul II reminded the Church that the mission of proclaiming the Gospel is incumbent on all of its members. Missionary activity, carried out in a wide variety of ways, is the task of all the Christian faithful (RM, no. 1).

The pope, noting that, historically, some churches arose out of lay missionary evangelization, reminded the Church that lay missionary effort is a consequence of baptismal dignity. Stressing the urgency of missionary evangelization, he said the lay faithful are obliged to witness to Christ's message of salvation in all circumstances, particularly in those where the institutional structure of the Church may be hindered (RM, no. 71).

The Holy Father described the sphere of lay missionary activity as "very extensive," pointing out that it encompasses various types of ecclesial services, functions, ministries, and ways of promoting the Christian life (RM, no. 72). Lay missionary endeavor can be expressed in diverse forms including lay missionary associations, international Christian volunteer organizations, ecclesial movements, groups, and sodalities of different kinds.

Within the ministry of evangelization, the Holy Father singled out lay catechists for particular recognition. He praised them as making "a singular and absolutely necessary contribution to the spread of the faith and the Church" (RM, no. 73). The pope observed that the ministry of lay catechists requires trained specialists capable of giving witness and communicating faith content. Because of the significance of the ministry, careful "doctrinal and pedagogical training, continuing spiritual and apostolic renewal, and a decent standard of living and social security must be assured" (RM, no. 73).

The encyclical's attention, however, was not restricted to catechists. The pope also praised those lay faithful who serve as "leaders of prayer, song and liturgy; leaders of basic ecclesial communities and Bible study groups; those in charge of charitable works; administrators of church resources; leaders in the various forms of the apostolate; religion teachers in schools" (RM, no. 74). The encyclical concludes with the pope's charge that all the laity "ought to devote part of their time to the Church" (RM, no. 74).

A Letter to Bishops on Some Aspects of the Church Understood as Communion
May 28, 1992

In a letter to the bishops of the Catholic Church, the Congregation for the Doctrine of the Faith sought to clarify the ecclesiology of communion. It did so by speaking of the Church as a mystery of communion based upon the concept of communion first articulated by the Second Vatican Council. Drawing upon the conciliar insight, the Congregation presented communion/*koinonia* as a "key for the renewal of Catholic ecclesiology."

The letter viewed communion not only as capable of explicating the relationship between God and humanity but also of the subsequent relationship existing within the Church. Communion, said the Congregation, spoke both to "the vertical (communion with God) and the horizontal (communion among men)" (SAC, 3). The Congregation found communion as suitable for expressing not only the mystery of the Church but clarifying the diversity of ministers within the Church.

Communion expresses the Church's nature both as sacrament and organically structured community. It allows the intrinsic unity of the Church to be understood, because ecclesial communion expresses both the visible and invisible dimensions of the Church. As an invisible reality, communion expresses the new relationship established with the Father through Christ in the Holy Spirit. This invisible reality is visibly manifest where the invisible communion with God is concretized through the visible ecclesial relationship expressed in "the teaching of the apostles, in the sacraments and in the hierarchical order" (SAC, no. 4).

Individuals introduced into this visible communion by faith and baptism remain in communion through the eucharist. The eucharist is the full expression and creative source of communion within the Church because "it unites each one of them [the baptized] with Christ himself" (SAC, 5) The visible sharing of "holy things" most powerfully concretized in the eucharist creates the invisible communion among the sharers (SAC, 6).

Having articulated the Church as a mystery of communion, the Congregation went on to examine the relationship between the universal Church and particular churches within the dynamic of communion. Citing the mutual interiority that the particular churches share with the universal Church, the letter insisted that "the universal Church is not the result of the communion of the churches, but in its essential mystery it is a reality ontologically and temporally prior to every individual particular church."

Appreciating the priority of the universal Church, the Congregation was careful not to reduce the particular churches to mere mediating agents. "From the point of view of the church understood as communion, the universal *communion of the faithful* and the *communion of the churches* are not consequences of one another but constitute the same reality seen from different viewpoints" (SAC, 10). The communion between the particular churches and the universal Church, rooted in faith and baptism, is based above all in the eucharist and the episcopate (SAC, 11). The oneness realized in the eucharistic body is the source of the oneness of the mystical body.

The unity of the Church is also rooted in the unity of the episcopal college maintained through the centuries by the apostolic succession and the petrine ministry. "The unity of the eucharist and the unity of the episcopate with Peter and under Peter are not independent roots of the unity of the Church, since Christ instituted the eucharist and the episcopate as essentially interlinked realities" (SAC, 14).

Ecclesial communion holds in positive tension all the various expressions of the unity and diversity in the Church. Knowing itself to be in communion with God and its various members gives the Church a healthy appreciation of its plurality. "This plurality refers both to the diversity of ministries, charisms and forms of life and apostolate within each particular church, and to the diversity of traditions in liturgy and culture among the various particular churches (SAC, 15).

Address to the Participants of the Symposium on the
Participation of the Laity in the Priestly Ministry
April 22, 1994

In an address three years ago to participants of a symposium called to examine the participation of the laity in the priestly ministry, John Paul II put the ministerial efforts of the lay faithful in the broader context of the overriding mission of the Church. He began by describing the life of the Church as a "mystery of missionary communion" (PSP, 1).

He characterized this organic communion as a "diversity and complementarity of vocations and states of life, of ministries, charisms and responsibilities as well as an intrinsic unity and mission involving all the baptized" (PSP, 1).

Situated within this organic unity is the lay apostolate as part of a divinely intended hierarchical structure. The development of the lay apostolate, noted the pope, is the occasion for "joyful gratitude" as it is "appropriately suited to the complex circumstances of the present day, which demand a renewed global missionary action" (PSP, 2).

This opportunity brings with it a responsibility for appropriate collaboration with priests. This collaboration of the lay faithful in the pastoral ministry begins with a correct appreciation of the "sacramental limits and the difference of charisms and ecclesial roles" (PSP, 2). Ministry, cautioned the pope, must always be understood in terms of relationship rather than function. He warned against a "functionalistic conception of holy orders, to the serious detriment of the theological identity of both the laity and the clergy, and consequently of the whole work of evangelization" (PSP, 2).

The well-being of the Church depends not upon "a haphazard infusion of energy" but on the reality that the Church is "joined and held together by every supporting ligament, with the proper functioning of each part" (PSP, 3). The proper acknowledgment, promotion, discernment, and coordination of individual gifts must occur "without confusing roles, functions or theological and canonical status" (PSP, 3).

The pope called for a careful balance of appreciation for the gifts of individual Christians and a proper discernment of a mentality of cultural and sociopolitical trends. "We cannot increase the communion and unity of the Church by 'clericalizing' the lay faithful or 'laicizing' priests" (PSP, 3). To foster ministry, the Church needs a healthy appreciation of "the diversity of vocations and states of life, the diversity of ministries, charisms and responsibilities."

A proper understanding of the participation of the laity in the pastoral ministry of priests requires a correct appreciation of the various meanings of ministry. The pope observed "that ministry has come to be employed not only for the *'officia'* and *'munera'* exercised as a consequence of orders but also in relation to the lay faithful in virtue of their baptismal identity" (PSP, 4). Misunderstanding can arise when the difference between baptismal priesthood and the ordained priesthood is confused or obscured. Such confusion also risks undermining the *proprium* of the laity (PSP, 4).

The ordained minister is the designated sacramental and pastoral representative. The services performed by him are those that are properly pastoral. The lay faithful may be entrusted with *officio* through deputation. However, deputation of *officio* in no way supplants the *munera* that properly belongs to the laity by their participation in the priesthood of Christ.

The ministry of Christ is the one source and constant reference for the ministry of the lay faithful. Ministry expresses the work by which the Church's members continue the "mission and ministry of Christ" within the Church and for the world (PSP, 4; cf. *Lumen Gentium*, no. 34). However, "only in virtue of ordination does ministry obtain that full univocal meaning that tradition has attributed" (PSP, 4).

The lay ministry, explained the pope, is rooted ontologically in the lay participation in Christ's priesthood and not in an ontological condition proper to pastors. Consequently, "if the pastors entrust them, in an extraordinary way, with some tasks ordinarily and properly connected with the pastoral ministry . . . lay people should know that these tasks are existentially rooted in their baptismal ministry" (PSP, 5).

The pope stressed that these ministerial distinctions do not stem from an attempt to defend clerical privilege but to respect the constitutive form Christ gave to the Church. The pope also emphasized that the "original subject" of the Church's mission is the entire ecclesial community. Therefore, the common apostolic responsibility of the baptized is not limited by ordained ministry but rather confirmed by it (PSP, 5).

The pope urged that the apostolate of the laity "be expanded in every way possible." This expansion need not conflict with the ontological nature of ordained ministry, for the two are properly ordered one to the other (PSP, 6).

Addendum

Marginal References

Religious and Human Promotion, John Paul II, April 28, 1978
"It is particularly to the laity by vocation and mission that the duty of promoting solidarity and justice within secular structures belongs. Their role in complementarity, especially in this area, will be above all by their witness and their contribution to an ever more adequate formation of the laity" (RHP, 10).

Lay Catholics in Schools: Witnesses to the Sacred, **Congregation for Catholic Education, October 15, 1982**
"Especially in the course of the last century, the authentic image of the laity within the People of God has become increasingly clear; it has now been set down in two documents of the Second Vatican Council, which give profound expression to the richness and uniqueness of the lay vocation: *The Dogmatic Constitution on the Church,* and the *Decree on the Apostolate of the Laity*" (LCS, 2).

"In a lay vocation, detachment and generosity are joined to legitimate defense of personal rights; but it is still a vocation, with the fullness of life and the personal commitment that the word implies. It offers ample opportunity for a life filled with enthusiasm" (LCS, 37).

"Religious formation must be oriented toward both personal sanctification and apostolic mission, for these are two inseparable elements in a Christian vocation. It is highly recommended, therefore, that all Catholics who work in schools, and most especially those who are educators, obtain the necessary qualifications by pursuing programs of religious formation in Ecclesiastical Faculties or in Institutes of Religious Science" (LCS, 65).

Libertatis Conscientia, **Congregation for the Doctrine of the Faith, March 22, 1986**
"It is not for the pastors of the Church to intervene directly in the political construction and organization of social life. This task forms

part of the vocation of the laity acting on their own initiative with their fellow citizens. They must fulfill this task conscious of the fact that the purpose of the Church is to spread the kingdom of Christ so that all men may be saved and that through them the world may be effectively ordered to Christ" (LB, 80).

Ex Corde Ecclesiae, John Paul II, August 15, 1990

"Lay people have found in university activities a means by which they too could exercise an important apostolic role in the Church. These lay Catholics are responding to the Church's call 'to be present, as signs of courage and intellectual creativity, in the privileged places of culture, that is, the world of education—school and university.' The future of Catholic universities depends to a great extent on the competent and dedicated service of lay Catholics" (ECE, 25).

Pastores Dabo Vobis, John Paul II, March 25, 1992

"Above all it is necessary that he be able to teach and support the laity in their vocation to be present in and to transform the world with the light of the Gospel, by recognizing this task of theirs and showing respect for it" (PDV, 59).

Directory on the Ministry and Life of Priests, Congregation for the Clergy, January 31, 1964

"One way to avoid falling into this 'democratistic' mentality is to shun the so-called clericalization of the laity, which tends to diminish the ministerial priesthood of the priest. After the Bishop, the term *pastor* can only be attributed in a proper and univocal sense to the priest by virtue of the ministerial priesthood received with Ordination. The attribute *pastoral,* in fact, refers both to the *potestas docendi et sanctificandi,* and to the *potestas regendi.* It should be remembered that these tendencies do not favor the true advancement of the laity because they frequently forget the authentic ecclesial vocation and mission of the laity in the world" (M&L, 19).

Documents on Lay Ministry from the National Conference of Catholic Bishops

Called and Gifted, **November 13, 1980**
On the fifteenth anniversary of *Apostolicam Actuositatem,* the U.S. bishops issued a pastoral letter to the Catholic laity entitled *Called and Gifted.* Drawing upon the conciliar model of the Church as the People of God, the bishops wished to affirm the conciliar recognition of the importance of the laity.

Called and Gifted focused on four specific calls to which the lay faithful are asked to respond: the call to adulthood; the call to holiness; the call to ministry; and the call to community.

The bishops described the call to ministry as arising out of baptism and confirmation. These two sacraments, asserted the bishops, "empower all believers to share in some form of ministry." The specific form of ministry is shaped according to individual gifts. Those individual gifts, however, are united in the one Body of Christ.

The bishops specifically recognized a relatively new development of "ecclesial ministers." These are lay individuals who participate in "professional ministry" in the Church. Ecclesial ministry, however, is not restricted to church professionals but includes volunteer and part-time workers.

Convinced that the laity make an indispensable contribution, the bishops look forward "to what is still to come under the guidance of the Holy Spirit." They committed themselves to making "those changes which will aid in building the kingdom."

Called and Gifted for the Third Millennium, **November 1995**
Fifteen years after *Called and Gifted* the U.S. bishops sought to update their initial reflections in light of subsequent church teaching, pastoral practice, and changing conditions. In this second document, the bishops acknowledged that the intervening fifteen years had seen a great increase in the number of lay faithful who minister in various ways within the Church.

The bishops noted numerous instances of professional part-time and volunteer ministry. These efforts enable the Church's mission to be carried forward. "All these actions, when performed in the name of Jesus and enacted under the aegis of the Church, are forms of ministry."

In assessing the challenges for the future, the bishops noted the importance of developing necessary resources to educate, train, and utilize lay ministers. However, they felt that the fundamental challenge was the "need to foster respectful collaboration, leading to mutual support in ministry, between clergy and laity."

Notes

1. *Lumen Gentium,* November 21, 1964.

2. Ibid.

3. Extraordinary Synod of Bishops *Final Report* (December 8, 1985) in *Origins* (December 19, 1985), 444–450.

4. Ibid.

5. Ibid.

6. Ibid.

7. Ibid.

8. Congregation for the Doctrine of the Faith, *Some Aspects of the Church Understood as Communion* (May 28, 1992).

9. Ibid.

10. *Catechism of the Catholic Church,* no. 234.

11. *Lumen Gentium.*

12. John Paul II, *General Audience Address* (September 27, 1989), no. 2.

13. Paul VI, *Apostolicam Actuositatem,* (November 18, 1965), no. 10.

14. John Paul II, *Christifideles Laici,* (December 11, 1994), no. 21.

15. Paul VI, *Evangelii Nuntiandi,* (December 8, 1975), no. 73.

Ecclesial Lay Ministry in a
Local Church BY MOST REV. JAMES T. HOFFMAN, D.D., J.C.L.

This paper begins with a review of the "explosion in lay ministry" over the last thirty years by citing the statistics for a single parish. It comments on the "signs of the times": a renewed awareness of the role of the laity, who are eager and well-educated; the emergence of new roles for women; the decline in the number of priests and religious; and the struggle to become a world Church. It includes the first-person stories of two among the approximately 6,000 persons who have participated in the diocesan ministry formation programs. It notes the development of the role of pastoral leaders and the significance of an ecclesiology of communion for reflecting on that role.

This paper also raises questions about the degree of emphasis given to teachings about the priesthood of the faithful, about the understanding of the difference between that and the priesthood of the ordained, and about the implications of that difference for questions of governance. An appendix lists twenty-five supervised ministries that were part of the diocesan ministry formation program in 1996–1997.

For those of us who cut our ministerial teeth on Catholic Action, especially the movements Young Christian Students, Young Christian Workers, and Christian Family Movement, the changes in ministry over the past thirty years have been dramatic. If in 1960, someone had suggested the breadth of lay leadership in our parish communities and diocesan structures as we experience it today, my response would have been one of disbelief. Yet, it is precisely the explosion in lay ministry that prompts this colloquium. To capture these past thirty years, I offer two snapshots.

SNAPSHOT I—CIRCA 1960

St. Peter's Parish, Mansfield, Ohio

Parishioners: 7,825	Mass Attendance: 4,565
Baptisms: 226	Converts: 57
Marriages: 61	Deaths: 69

Masses on Sunday: 5

Parish Staff: Pastor: 1; and Assistant Priests: 3
                      Organist: 1 (part time)

School Staff:

Grade School (1–8)	Students: 1,222	Staff: 14 religious/9 lay
High School (9–12)	Students: 437	Staff: 8 religious/11 lay

The ministry was straightforward: The women religious were responsible for the parochial elementary and secondary schools as well as the CCD program; the priests were responsible for the sacramental life, hospitals, nursing homes and homebound people, convert classes, marriage preparation, and CYO. The Laity were involved in St. Vincent de Paul Society, Serra Club and various fraternal groups. Simply speaking, the sisters did education and the priests celebrated the sacraments.

SNAPSHOT II—CIRCA 1993

St. Peter's Parish, Mansfield, Ohio (parish divided in 1969)

Parishioners: 6,245	Mass Attendance: 2,293
Baptisms: 110	Converts: 15
Marriages: 59	Deaths: 75

Masses on the Weekend: 6

| Parish/School Staff: | Pastor: 1; Associate Pastor: 1 |
| | (priest principal in high school) |

| Grade School (K–8) | Students: 472 | Staff: 47 lay/8 religious |
| High School (9–12) | Students 437 | |

New Positions:	Deacons: 3
	Pastoral Associates: 2 religious
	Director of Music (lay)
	Youth Minster (lay)
	Business Manager (lay)
	Montessori Director (lay)
	Child Care Director (lay)
	Public Relations/Development Director (lay)

At a glance, one can see that there have been some major shifts in these thirty years. The number of lay employees (are they all ecclesial lay ministers?) has grown from twenty-one in 1960 to fifty-three in 1993. Two obvious points would be that there has been significant staff development and a greater degree of specialization. The 1960 staff comprised generalists, religious and priests alike; the 1993 staff has special training as Montessori director, child care director, youth minister and business manager. In 1960, four priests were involved in the broad parish ministry; in 1993 two are generalists, and one serves as the high school principal. I do not believe that these developments were driven solely by the decline in the number of priests and religious.

Signs of the Times

In this interim, there was the Second Vatican Council, which was a breath of fresh air. The ecclesiology of *Lumen Gentium* brought new hope and new possibilities to all of us. Lay persons understood that they, too, were Church with a responsibility for the mission of Christ. They realized that their voice and their thoughts were important in the life of the Church. They rushed to participate in parish councils, school councils and the diocesan pastoral council. A new energy touched the life of the Church.

There were other elements: The adult Catholic community was both eager and well educated. There was the emergence of women in new roles in the Church. By 1980, the fact of fewer and aging religious and priests became a factor in the challenge of meeting the spiritual and human needs of the people. In these later years, there is a growing number of seekers—those who are searching for meaning in a comfortable and affluent society. In the midst of these developments, we experience the struggle to become a world Church—to address the issues of diversity, all the while aware of the polarization in our Church.

Ministry Formation

It was around 1970 when the Diocese of Toledo developed a game plan for the education and formation of lay ministers—Ministry Formation Programs (MFP). My estimate is that five to six thousand women and men have participated in MFP. The program has been revised at regular intervals. It is a five-year program in three segments: Year I, Years II and III, and Years IV and V. Graduates receive a certificate. The breadth of ministries is noted in the appendix.

The following stories speak about just two of these participants:

Helen is an educated lay woman who was active in the civic arena working with the poor and the street people, advocating for them, . . . and in her church community. She enrolled in the Ministry Formation Program to enrich her faith life. In Year II of the MFP, she became extremely ill and was diagnosed with a chronic illness. She was told to drop all her activities, but she had one more interview (out of five) to go to complete her Year II field education piece. She pushed up the meeting date of her visit to David's House (AIDS hospice) and changed the person she was to interview. As a result, she interviewed a women named Agnes Gray, who, in listening to her story, saw the gifts and talents that a trained AIDS minister needed and invited her to participate in this ministry. She has been at it ever since. Her pastor and community have affirmed her in this and have put her gifts and talents to work in the parish as well.

Allow Jeannine to tell her story. "It was my experience that I felt a call, responded to the call, and discovered my need for formation. As I received formation, I discovered a call to respond to the declining numbers of priests and felt led to get my master's degree. Through my response, I moved through a process which led me from being a Sunday School teacher, adult educator, parish leader of various ministries, DRE, theology teacher, Adult Continuing Formation to Lead Agent for Pastoral Planning in the Diocese of Toledo."

Helen's and Jeannine's stories are legion in youth ministry, prison ministry, RCIA leadership, marriage preparation, catechetical ministry, et al.

Among the fruits of the Second Vatican Council, the ones that bring me most hope are the development of lay ministry and the Rite of Christian Initiation of Adults. This is not to say all is well. There are concerns about the issue of collaboration between clergy and laity, the issue of just compensation, and the matter of personnel policy.

Pastoral Leaders

However, picking up on Father Heft's sentence, "We need to understand not only the authority ELM can and should exercise, but also how that authority is granted, and by whom" (par. 19, p. 9).

For fourteen years, the Diocese of Toledo has encouraged the role of pastoral leader, a.k.a. parish life coordinator, parish administrator, et al. I am referring to that person responsible for the oversight of a parish community in keeping with canon 517, par. 2. Presently, eleven of our one hundred sixty-three parishes are under the care of a pastoral leader. Those selected have been women religious, deacons, and a lay man. Our experience with this model of pastoral care brings with it a number of ecclesiological considerations. In the life of the Church, there was a shift occurring from the point where the reflections on the ministerial role of the laity were seen through the lenses of the hierarchical image of Church to the post-conciliar point where the image of Church as communion is brought to bear upon these same reflections.

In the Apostolic Exhortation on the Laity, *Christifideles Laici*, John Paul II expands on the whole notion of the laity being sharers in the priestly, prophetic, and kingly mission of Jesus Christ. He concludes the section by saying,

The participation of the lay faithful and the three-fold mission of Christ as Priest, Prophet and King finds its source in the anointing of Baptism, its further development in Confirmation and its realization and dynamic sustenance in the Holy Eucharist. It is a participation given to each member of the lay faithful individually, inasmuch as each is one of the many who form the one Body of the Lord: in fact, Jesus showers his gifts upon the Church, which is his body and his Spouse. In such a way, individuals are sharers in the threefold mission of Christ, in virtue of their being members of the Church, as St. Peter clearly teaches, when he defines the baptized as "a chosen race, a royal priesthood, a holy nation, God's own people" (1 Pt 2:9). Precisely because it derives from *Church* communion, *the sharing of the lay faithful in the three-fold mission of Christ requires that it be lived and realized* in communion *and* for the increase of communion itself (Christifideles Laici, no. 14).

The ecclesiology of communion is the central and fundamental idea of the council's documents. The *Final Report* of the Extraordinary Synod of Bishops, 1985, reminded us that

"Koinonia/*communion, founded on Sacred Scripture, have been held in great honor in the early Church and in the Eastern Churches to this day. Thus, much was done by the Second Vatican Council so that the Church as* communion *might be more clearly understood and concretely incorporated into life. What does the complex word communion mean? Fundamentally, it is a matter of communion with God through Jesus Christ in the sacraments. Baptism is the door and the foundation of communion in the Church. The eucharist is the source and the culmination of the whole Christian life. The communion of the eucharistic Body of Christ signifies and produces, that is, builds up, the intimate communion of all the faithful in the Body of Christ which is the Church* (Extraordinary Synod II, C. 1).

Some Questions

It is my sense that we are yet to tap into the full possibilities of the priesthood of the faithful, those fully initiated into the Body of Christ by baptism, confirmation, and the eucharist. A more balanced understanding of Church, especially Church as communion, should inspire our thinking about ELM. Does Church as communion provide a different insight to ELM than Church as hierarchical?

From these reflections, I raise the following questions:

1. Have we emphasized the conciliar teaching adequately as it shows forth the priesthood of the faithful? Does this teaching expand the possibilities for ministry in the Catholic Church? Are we somewhat reluctant in reclaiming the full understanding of the priesthood of the faithful, lest it seem to impinge on the ministry of the ordained? The area of preaching might be cited as an example. The homily at Mass is reserved to the ordained. Some in our presbyterate would not be a parish chaplain who serves under a pastoral leader.

2. Another question is how do we understand the difference between the common priesthood of the faithful and the ordained priesthood? What is the fundamental meaning of "though they differ essentially and not only in degree . . . ?" (LG, no. 10) Has the post-conciliar reflection provided us with any deeper understanding of that phrase and of the difference between ordained priesthood and priesthood of the faithful? Both must share responsibility for the mission of Christ. That seems clear enough as long as we use a broad phrase for the mission of Christ as "to spread the Gospel throughout the world."

Yet, it seems to be less clear when we begin to look at particular ministries. For example, is there something about this distinction between the two priesthoods that prevents a baptized person from oversight of a parish community? Is that a role that can only be performed by an ordained person?

Conjoined to that consideration, we have the issue of governance, a.k.a. jurisdiction. Can the pastoral leader alienate church property, or is that only to be done by the canonical pastor? When can the pastoral leader delegate a visiting priest to witness a marriage?

In the 1950s, it was my understanding that the power of governance flowed from the power of orders. I have been told that this was not the case in the earliest centuries of the Church, but it became the reality in the Middle Ages. Has there been a developing theology since the Second Vatican Council that separates these two realities of governance and orders? What are the implications for ecclesial lay ministry of canon 129, par. 2, "Lay members of the Christian faithful can cooperate in the exercise of this power in accord with the norm of law?"

In a recent report entitled *"Creating a Home,"* the LCWR Executive Committee offered a series of recommendations. They indicated that in offering the recommendations for action, they also admitted a degree of frustration. "By initiating this project, the Executive Committee had hoped to discover new avenues through which women could play more significant roles in Church. However, the project has made clear to us that as long as jurisdiction (the power to govern) is tied to ordination, a very limited number of roles with authority will be open to women. The relationship of jurisdiction to ordination creates a glass ceiling for women in the Church. This seems markedly inconsistent with recent pledges made by the Church to involve women in governance and to advance the cause of women" (*"Creating a Home,"* LCWR Special Report, p. 85).

Conclusion

There is a host of other issues that might arise at the colloquium. For example, What steps might be taken to enable a more effective collaboration between ecclesial lay ministers and priests? Do we need a better way of providing formation for ministry? How do we address a host of issues in regard to personnel procedures such as conflict resolution or contracts?

I think if there was more clarity on our ecclesiology and our sacramental theology, we might be able to handle the practical concerns more effectively. Perhaps the issues mentioned above will be helpful to our conversation.

This paper has attempted to focus on two issues:

1. Do the conciliar and post-conciliar teachings on the sacraments of initiation and a communion ecclesiology contain ministerial possibilities that enrich our theology of lay ministry?

2. Has the teaching on the priesthood of the faithful undergone developments since the Second Vatican Council that bear on ecclesial lay ministry? Have we not experienced some new directions in the area of governance?

Appendix

Diocese of Toledo
Ministry Formation Program, 1996–1997
Supervised Ministries

Abused Children	1
Aids	1
Adult Education/Formation	4
Befrienders	2
Bereavement	2
Bible Study	1
Elementary Formation	1
Evangelization	1
Family Life	4
Hispanic Ministry	1
Hospital Visitation (informal)	2
Liturgy	5
Ministry of Care	1
Montessori Religious Education	1
Parish Nurse	2
Pastoral Care in Hospital (formal)	5
Prison	1
RCIA	8
Recovery	1
Religious Education (all forms)	10
Remembering	1
Rural Life	1
Retrouvaille	2
Small Faith Groups	3
Youth (teens)	6

Reflections on the Experience of Ecclesial Lay Ministry

BY MOST REV. HOWARD J. HUBBARD, D.D.

This paper opens with a review of the commitment of the Diocese of Albany to make the promotion of collaborative ministry its number one priority—a commitment implemented by the development of a broad continuum of educational and formational opportunities and of a diocesan policy that specifies how these opportunities are to be financed. It proposes a definition of ecclesial lay ministry based on diocesan experience and reviews the nomenclature used by the diocese for the nonordained in parish ministry, noting the human resource issues that need to be considered.

This paper comments on the tension of living with two coexisting principles in our Vatican II Church: the common dignity and equality among all members of the Church, and the hierarchical nature of the Church. It concludes with four cautions/concerns crystallized by the papers of Dr. Zeni Fox and Father James Heft.

In the Diocese of Albany, we have been seeking to promote the ministry that belongs to all the faithful by virtue of baptism, confirmation, and eucharist. In two pastoral letters *We Are His People* (1978) and *We Are God's Priestly People* (1988), which have served as the vision statements during my twenty years as bishop, the ideas of collegiality, collaboration, and shared responsibility have been the predominant themes.

We have presented a broad understanding of lay ministry, reflecting the vision of *Christifideles Laici* and echoed in *Called and Gifted for the Third Millennium*, that "through the sacraments of baptism, confirmation, and eucharist every Christian is called to participate actively and co-responsibly in the Church's mission of salvation in the world.

Moreover, in those same sacraments, the Holy Spirit pours out gifts which make it possible for every Christian man and woman to assume different ministries and forms of service that complement one another and are for the good of all" (*Christifideles Laici*, no. 20, and *Called and Gifted for the Third Millennium*, p. 15).

> *While carefully drawing the distinction between the common priest-hood of the faithful and the ministerial or hierarchical priesthood, which is rooted in the apostolic succession and vested in the power and responsibility of the ordained to act in the person of Christ, we have also recognized that these modes of participation in the priesthood of Christ are ordered to one another so that the ministerial priesthood is at the service of the common priesthood and directed to the unfolding of the baptismal grace of all Christians* (Catechism of the Catholic Church, 1547).

Hence, we have tried to point out that each of us by virtue of baptism has the right and the responsibility to participate in Christ's saving mission of praising and worshiping the Lord, of teaching God's word, of serving God's people, and of building up the kingdom here on earth in preparation for the fullness of life together in the kingdom of heaven.

We emphasize that this responsibility of being about the work of Christ's Church is ours, regardless of our state in life or the differing roles we may actually exercise. We are all called to be co-creators with God, advancing the Lord's kingdom in our day. Every person's contribution is vitally needed so that together, in a rich diversity, we can build up the Christian community by enhancing the sacredness and growth of others.

These themes have been promoted further through our diocesan vision statement, "We are God's People sharing a responsibility to witness to God's unconditional love and to bring the healing presence of Christ to our world"; and in a video *We Are All God's Priestly People* that has been shown in our parishes as well as on all the local cable-access stations within our fourteen-county diocese. All of the vehicles I have cited make it clear that the call to ministry on the part of the laity must not be perceived as a luxury or concession but as the consequence of the rights and responsibilities that belong to every baptized member of God's priestly people.

In order to implement this vision of a universally ministering Church, we have adopted the promotion of collaborative ministry as our number one diocesan priority. This priority is rooted in the recognition that collaborative ministry is not something that just happens. It must be articulated clearly so that everyone understands the vision; it must be prepared for carefully, so that people, especially in leadership, have the skills to function in such a model; and, therefore, it must be nurtured and implemented patiently and sensitively.

Our ordained ministers and other parish staff—lay and religious—are the key for promoting this vision and its implementation at the local level. If they are to do this well, however, they not only must understand the theology of collaborative ministry but also must learn the skills of ministering themselves in a collaborative fashion and of enabling others to do so. In other words, if the diocesan and parish leadership do not function in a collaborative fashion, in other words, it is most unlikely that the wider ecclesial community will gain this facility. Therefore, we have undertaken the following two steps to foster collaborative ministry in our diocese:

> **First,** the development of a broad continuum of educational and formational opportunities to assist those desiring to minister, with the initial and ongoing education and formation resources they will require to serve well.

> **Second,** although it is implicit in the previous point, the formation of an overall diocesan policy or guidelines that specify who or which church entity finances these educational and formational opportunities. If we are serious about collaborative ministry, we must be equally serious about assisting the laity to meet the expenses associated with their education and formation.

Presently, the diocese and parishes are bearing the cost for our Formation for Ministry program and the various certification programs that are available. The degreed program offered by St. Bernard's Institute—a postgraduate program of studies offering a master's in theology and other related ecclesial disciplines for the clergy, religious, and laity of the diocese—is financed equally by the diocese, parish, and participants, with scholarships available for participants unable to finance their portion of the program. What remains lacking, however, is any program to assist people seeking an undergraduate degree in preparation for ministry prior to their employment with some church entity, as well as established policies for financing the postgraduate studies offered in institutions other than the diocesan-sponsored St. Bernard's Institute program.

Our experience, to date, shows that efforts to promote collaborative ministry only beget further ministry. The peer-to-peer ministry of the laity, in particular, is bearing rich fruits in our diocese. By modeling lay ministry, by sharing their stories of being called to ministry, and by inviting others to an awareness of the Spirit in their lives, lay ministers—both salaried and volunteer—have been a wonderful resource for recruiting, supporting, and affirming other laity in the acceptance of new ministerial roles. For example, many of the laity who have completed our Formation for Ministry program have enabled others to serve as parish retreat leaders or leaders of small faith sharing and Scripture study groups; as members of bereavement, hospitality, youth, young adult and social action committees; as participants on AIDS care teams or on retreat teams for those in local jails and state prisons or for those with developmental disabilities; and as people willing to share with the wider community their professional expertise in areas such as counseling of the unemployed, assisting immigrants with legal problems and language skills, and offering medical and nursing care in parish or school-based health programs.

Furthermore, these efforts seem to be responsive to the signs of the times: the deep hunger for spirituality and a more in-depth understanding of the Scriptures; the declining number of ordained and vowed ministers; the rising aspirations of women; the growing dehumanization and depersonalization within our society; the alienation and disaffiliation of generation X; and the widening gap between the "have's" and the "have not's" within our society.

I cite this brief overview of our lived experience in seeking to promote lay ministry and the concepts of collaboration or shared responsibility in the Diocese of Albany as the context for my reading of and reflection upon the papers presented by Dr. Zeni Fox and Father James Heft, SM.

The data reported by Dr. Fox in her paper "Ecclesial Lay Ministry" very much reflect the reality experienced in the Diocese of Albany, especially the explosion of lay ministry since the late 1960s, the difference of nomenclature being employed throughout the diocese, and the preponderance of women exercising these expanding roles. However, as a diocese, we have not developed formally or explicitly a definition of ecclesial lay ministry. Our emphasis has been on the baptismal call to holiness and ministry extended to all the faithful and on formulating policies and programs that facilitate this vision. In other words, as a diocese, we have not addressed directly the question to be considered by the colloquium, namely, what is to be included in ecclesial lay ministry (i.e., the participation and service to the community as such by some of the baptized) and what should be seen as a part of lay ministry broadly conceived (i.e., the participation in the mission that is given by baptism to all the faithful in our diocese). However, there is no question about the fact that we have been dealing with the reality of what is being described as ecclesial lay ministry, and this experience offers some insights that may be of help in addressing this critical question.

The description of lay ministry that Father Thomas O'Meara, OP, offers resonates best with our experience and offers a good starting point for defining ecclesial lay ministry. His definition states: "Christian ministry is the public activity of a baptized follower of Jesus Christ flowing from the Spirit's charism and an individual personality on behalf of a Christian community to witness to, serve and realize the kingdom of God."[1]

It would seem that this definition of Christian ministry could be nuanced to describe or define ecclesial lay ministry if it were phrased as follows: "Ecclesial lay ministry is the public activity of a baptized follower of Jesus Christ flowing from an inner awareness of one's baptismal call and of a responsiveness to the Spirit's charism and authorized or commissioned by the bishop or his delegate in direct service to the community of faith."

Such a definition highlights three dimensions or aspects of ecclesial lay ministry that distinguish it from lay ministry broadly conceived. First, it stresses the idea of vocation: that this ministry is a response to a genuine call from God and is not to be perceived as a practical necessity imposed by the current shortage of priests and religious nor as motivated by some kind of an American desire to democratize the Church. Furthermore, this definition underscores that the minister must be exercising the activity with a clear understanding that such activity is in response to his or her baptismal call to ministry and to the gifts, talents, and charism with which he or she has been endowed by the Spirit. Without this awareness, the individual's activity may be directed to building up the faith community, but would it truly be ecclesial ministry? For example, the teacher in the Catholic school who is there solely because he or she needs a job is exercising a service directed to building up the life of the Church, but can this activity truly be a ministry if there is no sense of call or vocation on the part of the individual?

Second, this definition indicates that some form of authorization or *deputation* by the bishop or his delegate (e.g., pastor, pastoral life director, or diocesan official) is necessary for this to be a truly ecclesial ministry. This dimension appears necessary to ensure that there has been an appropriate assessment of the competency on the part of the individual to perform the public activity, as well as of the person's character, formation, and good standing within the faith community. For while the individual's sense of call and mission is an important dimension in ecclesial lay ministry, so too is the Church's discernment or judgment that the lay person is suitable and qualified to exercise a public ministry on behalf of the faith community, similar to the assessment made by the Church on candidates for the priesthood and religious life. Such an assessment need not exclude the role of the wider ecclesial community in this discernment, as will be suggested later.

Third, this definition reflects the fact that the activity to be exercised has been evaluated by some ecclesiastical authority as being directed to the inner life of the Church as such, and, thus, as being a *bona fide* ecclesial lay ministry as distinguished from that activity involved in witnessing to Christ in the family, the community, and the marketplace.

This proposed definition is flexible enough to allow the term "ecclesial lay ministry" to be applied both to professionals who are employed by the church and to volunteers as well as to those who exercise this as a lifelong ministry or for a limited period of time—the distinguishing characteristic not being salary, compensation, or longevity but rather the possession of the knowledge, skills, and personal characteristics required to perform the particular public task designated by the church.

Our experience in the local church, however, has led us to conclude, as I believe the establishment of the NCCB Subcommittee on Lay Ministry also reflects, that the development of lay ministry—mostly salaried and at the parish level—requires a more careful assessment of what is happening both with regard to the activities being performed and the nomenclature being employed so that there will be greater clarity and uniformity throughout the diocese with regard to the terminology being utilized, the expected competencies required, and the relationship of these ministers to the local church.

A task force consisting of clergy, religious, and laity was established to study the issue and, after broad consultation throughout the diocese and a study of trends throughout the country, it determined that nonordained ministers serving in parish ministry be classified in one of three categories: parish life director, pastoral associate, and pastoral minister.

The parish life director is defined as a professional minister who is appointed by the diocesan bishop as a leader of a parish or a cluster of parishes. In collaboration with the canonical pastor, the parish life director has the responsibility of overseeing the entire Catholic community in a specific locale. She or he enables and empowers the community to be a sign of Christ's healing presence.

The pastoral associate is described as a professional minister, usually full time, who is responsible for a specific area of pastoral life under the direction of the pastor or parish life director. This title of pastoral associate is distinct from that of associate pastor, who is an ordained priest sharing responsibility with the bishop, local pastor, and the parish staff for building up the kingdom through the Christian community. The title of pastoral associate may further be delineated as pastoral associate for faith formation, liturgy, pastoral care/social outreach, or youth ministry.

The pastoral minister is seen as a volunteer minister. She or he gives service in a specific area of parish life under the direction of the pastor the or parish life director, the associate pastor, or the pastoral associate.

In this schema, the bishop directly appoints the pastor, the pastoral life director, and the associate pastor. The pastoral associate and the parish minister are appointed by the pastor or the parish life director, who is expected to follow the criteria developed by the diocese in ensuring that the minister has the knowledge, skills, experience, and character to fulfill the respective pastoral position. In this regard, it has been noted that many of the academic institutions preparing laity for ministry in the church do not offer a full course in Catholic theology and often do not address formational issues. Until this situation changes, the diocese must bear the responsibility to ensure that lay ministers are properly conversant with Catholic theology and tradition and must provide programs for initial and ongoing formation and spiritual development. It should be noted, as well, that while this more academic model of preparation and formation is presently the one being utilized in our diocese, some members of the task force have suggested that an alternative approach to formation, that of mentoring, service, and learning, such as exists in many monastic communities, might also prove beneficial.

This study also underscored the need for clear policy and guidelines addressing the recruitment and interviewing of prospective ministers, the development of well-defined job descriptions and ministerial agreements, the formulation of wages and benefits, and the establishment of evaluation and grievance procedures. While such have been available through our diocesan human resources office, it is evident that more work needs to be done to enable pastors and other individuals involved in the hiring of lay ministers to understand to a greater degree the importance of following these policies and guidelines, and to help them in developing the practical skills they need, especially in the area of recruitment and supervision.

Most of our pastors—and those who assist them with this responsibility—frequently have not had much training or experience in exercising these responsibilities. At the diocesan level, we have a panel of clergy, religious, and laity who assist the bishop in the screening of candidates for ordained ministry, monitor the progress of such candidates during their formation, and make recommendations to the bishop concerning their readiness or suitability for ordination. It would seem that a similar panel could assist the pastor or other hiring agent at the parish level and, in so doing, provide a greater involvement of the parish community in discerning a person's call and suitability for ecclesial lay ministry.

Further, experience dictates that our lay ministers be apprised fully of their rights as church employees or volunteers and know the recourse they have to address grievances either through our human resources office or through the diocesan administrative review process. Unfortunately, many lay ministers find themselves serving at the whim of the pastor, especially when a change in pastors takes place. It is imperative, therefore, that both the pastor and the lay minister be informed fully about their roles, rights, and responsibilities. Very often, problems can be averted both for pastors and for lay ministers through consultation with the diocesan human resources office or with other appropriate diocesan offices (e.g., schools, religious education, prayer and worship, Catholic Charities, and pastoral planning) prior to action being taken or grievances initiated.

It would seem, as well, that this establishment of clear diocesan guidelines and nomenclature, ministerial criteria, hiring protocol, evaluation procedures, and grievance mechanisms would do much to preserve the necessary distinctions between the ordained and nonordained articulated in the Vatican Instruction: Questions Regrading Collaboration of Nonordained Faithful in Priests' Sacred Ministry[2] and to guard against the development of a congregational mentality or to combat the lack of relationships between ecclesial lay ministers and the diocese, which our own experience in Albany and the observations of others raise as a potentially serious concern.[3]

Moreover, our experience is that, while there are tensions that lay ministers have in their relationships with pastors and other church authorities, it should be noted that these tensions are not unique to the ecclesial lay minister. Frequently, the very same tensions are experienced by ordained priests serving in the role of associate pastor or by deacons. This observation is not intended to minimize the problems and tensions but to put them in a broader context that perceives these tensions not so much as a clergy versus laity or an ordained versus nonordained struggle but as an issue of how authority is perceived and exercised in the Church: hierarchically or collegially; bureaucratically or collaboratively.

Many of these tensions arise, I would suggest, from two very important theological principles that coexist in our Vatican II Church. On the one hand, the Second Vatican Council emphasizes the common dignity and equality that exists among all the members of God's people. All, therefore, are called to the same holiness of life, and all are entitled to become engaged actively in exercising the Church's mission to the world. On the other hand, the council also highlights the hierarchical nature of the Church. We live as believers within a Church that has an appointed structure with predetermined ranks of authority.

These two notions—so evident in the conciliar documents and in the revised Code of Canon Law—are not contradictory, but they do create a tension when it comes to such practical things as how decisions get made in the church or to when and how one is accountable. This tension is real at the level of the universal Church, and it also affects our local church and our parish communities.

For the immediate future, then, we are faced with the challenge of living with this tension, with these two differing notions. One side stresses our unity with Christ Jesus and with one another; the other side stresses the need for organization, structure, and authority. One side acknowledges the gifts of God that exist within individual believers; the other side stresses the diversity of functions and roles that must be lived out within the Christian community. Somewhere in between, we are expected to govern and to be governed; to minister and to be ministered to. The challenge, then, is to recognize the authority of those who hold pastoral office within the church without diminishing the value of those ecclesial lay ministers who recognize their call to share leadership responsibility arising from baptism, confirmation, and the eucharist.

The style of interaction among the ecclesial lay minister, the pastor, the parish, and the bishop must, therefore, be seen within the context of this creative tension. It must flow from an understanding of the fact that before any distinction of roles or office in the church, we stand as one family of the baptized and that it is the exercise of the collaborative priesthood of the baptized that most fully continues the sacramental presence of Christ in the world.

This understanding demands an interdependence and partnership between bishop and priest; among clergy, religious, and laity; and between parish and diocese. Bishops, priests, deacons, and ecclesial lay ministers have a serious responsibility to help all the members of the Church to discover, to develop, and to use their God-given gifts, talents, and charisms for the well-being of our church and society. The laity have an equally serious responsibility to rediscover the scriptural revelation about the priesthood of all the faithful and the common vocation to holiness and ministry that they possess by virtue of baptism. Such an understanding of Church, therefore, emphasizes that the Church is not a stratified or a clerically dominated society but a community of persons, all sharing in the priesthood of Jesus Christ and all called equally to be the People of God.

Such an understanding stresses, furthermore, that the Church is a community of collaborative ministry, that is, a community in which each member is challenged to see his or her baptism as a call to holiness and ministry; a community that seeks to help its members to discern the personal charisms given to them by the Spirit and to enable them to employ their gifts in the mission of the Church; a community whose ordained, vowed, and ecclesial lay ministers see the fostering of greater participation in the work of the Church and the building up of the kingdom as essential to their responsibility as leaders.

In summary, then, the theological model employed in our diocese envisions that responsibility for the mission of the Church is collaborative and shared by all the baptized—ordained, vowed, and lay—all bound together by a variety of gifts and ministries and all interacting dynamically in a supportive, affirming, and complementary way to accomplish the mission of Jesus in our day. Some within the church community (the ordained, the vowed, and the ecclesial lay ministers, be they salaried or volunteer) are called to exercise this responsibility for ministry by building up the inner life of the Church—the Body of Christ; others are called to exercise this responsibility by building up the kingdom of God through their service to family, community, and world. This understanding of ministry does not negate the unique and distinctive role of the ordained minister, the evangelical charism of the vowed, or the sterling gifts of the ecclesial lay minister; but it underscores, as Archbishop William Borders points out so well in his pastoral letter *You Are a Royal Priesthood*, that "before any distinction of roles or offices in the church, we stand as one family of the baptized. It is the community as a whole to whom is given the primary responsibility for the mission of the church, and it is the whole community which stands as the first minister of the kingdom."[4]

In conclusion, I would raise certain cautions or concerns crystallized by the papers on ecclesial lay ministry presented by Dr. Zeni Fox and Father James Heft, SM.

First, there is a concern that the search to understand and to define a theology of ecclesial lay ministry seems to be very parish-focused. Dr. Fox acknowledges that "most of the sociological research that has been done studies ecclesial lay ministers working in parishes."[5] While this focus is understandable because it is in the parish where there has been such phenomenal explosion of lay ministries, it is critically important, I believe, that we do not ignore or overlook the roles the laity have exercised traditionally in our Catholic schools, religious education offices, colleges and universities, charities, and health care institutions—roles that not only continue but also indeed have expanded with the declining numbers of ordained and vowed ministers serving in these apostolates. Especially, given the emphasis that many dioceses and religious communities are placing on developing a strong sense of mission and Catholic identity among board members and staffs who oversee these apostolates, many of the laity serving in these Catholic institutions, as well as the laity serving in non-Catholic institutions (e.g., as Catholic chaplains in colleges, hospitals, jails, and nursing homes) perceive themselves as ecclesial lay ministers as much as the laity who minister in our parishes. It is important, then, that we not exclude laity serving in extraparochial ministries from our consideration of who qualifies as an ecclesial lay minister.

A second concern is that, in defining ecclesial lay ministry, we not do so in a way that fosters a new clericalism or that relegates the laity who are not defined as ecclesial lay ministers to the status of second-class citizenship or of persons having a lesser call within the Church. Historically, we have tended to do this with clergy and religious, seeing them as the doers and the activists in the Church, and looking upon ordination or religious profession as elevating people to a status of spiritual superiority; whereas, the laity have been seen as exercising a more modest, passive role in the church community and in no way competing with the clergy and religious in theology and spirituality.

It is interesting to note that this concern about the clericalization of some lay ministers was cited by the Latin American bishops in their 1996 meeting on Lay Ministers in the New Evangelization.[6] Ecclesial lay ministry, then, should not be defined or promoted in a way that presents the persons exercising such ministries as having a better or more noble call than other laity who do not exercise ministries geared to serving the faith community as such.

Third, akin to the preceding concern is the tendency we have had in the church, especially since the Second Vatican Council, to focus on the development of ecclesial ministries, almost to the detriment or exclusion of the laity's call to ministry in the world. The ministerial section of the bishops' 1980 pastoral *Called and Gifted,* for example, speaks first about the laity's role and responsibility to bring Christian values and practices to bear upon complex questions such as those of business ethics, political choice, economic security, quality of life, and cultural development and to be an extension of the Church's redeeming presence in the world. It is not until after the laity's normative secular ministry is affirmed that the bishops speak about the call of the laity to ecclesial or church ministry. What *Called and Gifted* offers, then, is an inclusive view of lay ministry, wherein the laity's church service is seen as ministry but so also their everyday life and work, and preeminently so.

As Bishop Raymond Lucker pointed out, however, in an address to the National Conference of Catholic Bishops at Collegeville, Minnesota, in June 1986 entitled "Linking Church and World," we have tended to reverse the order outlined in *Called and Gifted,* calling the laity first to ministries within the Church and then, secondarily, or at least with far less emphasis, to ministries for the transformation of society. It is critically important, therefore, that in defining ecclesial lay ministry, we not do so in a way that de-emphasizes or detracts from the vital and indispensable role the laity have in the home, on the job, and in the neighborhood, the community, and the marketplace to be about the transformation of society and to make the gospel message real in the family, in social life, in business transactions, and in the world of politics.

The final concern to be noted, in light of the previous observations, is that it may be premature to describe with definitiveness ecclesial lay ministry. As Father Heft observes, "The outline of ministerial activities found in the New Testament reflects a dynamism and a creativity, as well as a need for a certain order and coordination . . . this dynamism and creativity ought to be understood as ongoing."[7]

Certainly, as the colloquium on ecclesial lay ministry suggests, there is need at this juncture in the history of the Church in the United States to examine the explosion of new lay ministries within the Church and, based upon the experience of the past three decades, to effect a certain order and coordination. This reflection is crucially important lest we get too far down the road in development of patterns and relationships that may not be truly reflective of sound theology and discipline within the framework of our Catholic Christian tradition.

The endeavor, then—to develop some preliminary practical disposition about who qualifies for the designation as an ecclesial lay minister and about what is the foundation of that person's responsibility and accountability within the local church—will be of extreme benefit as well as an enormous contribution to the life of the contemporary Church. However, just as it took several centuries for the order of bishop, presbyter, and deacon to become defined fully, it would seem that the present effort to define ecclesial lay ministry, while needed and appropriate, should remain tentative. In other words, while it is imperative that we study, reflect, clarify, and theologize about ecclesial lay ministry, at this point in history, we ought not to attempt to finalize what is still a developing reality.

Notes

1. Thomas Franklin O'Meara, OP, *Theology of Ministry* (Ramsey, N.J.: Paulist Press, 1983), p. 142.

2. "Eight Vatican Offices/Instruction, Some Questions Regarding Collaboration of Nonordained Faithful in Priests' Sacred Ministry" in *Origins* 27:24.

3. See Philip J. Murnion, *New Parish Ministers: Laity & Religious on Parish Staffs* (New York: National Pastoral Life Center), p. 130; Zeni Fox, "A Post-Vatican II Phenomenon; Lay Ministers: A Critical Three-Dimensional Study," unpublished dissertation (Fordham University, 1986), pp. 204, 211–212.

4. William Borders, "You Are a Royal Priesthood," in *Origins* 18:11, p. 170.

5. Zeni Fox, "Ecclesial Lay Ministers," p. 4.

6. Latin American Meeting on Lay Ministries in the New Evangelization, Caracas, Venezuela (March 15–17, 1996), p. 23.

7. Father James Heft "Toward a Theology of Ecclesial Lay Ministry," p. 30.

Colloquium Questions

*Note: Participants read the papers before the colloquium opened and for-
mulated questions for discussion at the colloquium. The questions were
then grouped by the staff for small-group discussion. Many questions
appeared in more than one group. Here, each question appears only once.*

Group A: An Appropriate and Adequate Definition of Ecclesial Lay Ministry

1. Does the reality of the "new ministers" (Murnion's language) call
   for an "ordering" by the official church? If yes, is there within this
   reality a single group, "ecclesial lay ministers"? Or multiple groups
   (cf. CELAM)? How is/are members of such (a) group(s) to be
   defined/delineated?

2. Is the definition of ecclesial lay ministers given in our preparatory
   material ("Those lay men and women, including vowed religious,
   who have been prepared professionally for specific roles of leadership in and for the church") appropriate or adequate? Is there a technical and logically complete definition of lay ministry that we can all
   accept? Is there a difference between church employees and lay ministers?

3. Is there any difference between those who volunteer to participate in
   lay ministry and those who are paid to be lay ministers? Does this
   lead to differing notions of ministry?

4. How can a theology of ecclesial lay ministry be developed without
   clarification of the theology of all ministry within and outside the
   institutional Church? That is, is ecclesial lay ministry any more a
   calling and/or a vocation than nursing, teaching, or social work?

5. An issue: the relationship and tensions between ELM as vocation and profession need to be explored more fully.

6. What are the sources (*fontes*) of lay ministry, and what is the relationship between the sources?

7. What are the character and the scope of the governing responsibility of ELM?

8. What aspects of ELM transcend ecclesiological/theological differences? How can these be capitalized on?

9. How to define ministry: lay ministry vis-à-vis priestly ministry, the ministry of the baptized vis-à-vis the ministry of the ordained—a question of degree or of kind?

10. What is the true theological definition of ecclesial lay ministry? What are the factors and the determinants that are essential to ecclesial lay ministry? We really need to clarify with some precision what is required for genuine ecclesial lay ministry. When everything is ministry, nothing is ministry.

11. Is the definition of *ecclesial* lay ministry as set by the colloquium a useful one? For what reason is *ecclesial* added to lay? What does it clarify? What questions does it raise?

Group B: Relationship of the Baptized and the Ordained in Light of the Needs and Mission of the Church

1. If ministry is understood more in terms of relationships than functions, how are stewardship, responsibility, and accountability determined?

2. Given the "relational" nature of all forms of ministry, is the current self-understanding of ordained ministry conducive to a continued flourishing of ELM?

3. Should the new ministers be understood as properly lay, or should they be ordained?

4. Is the tension between lay ministers and pastors due not only to the dialectical situation within the Church of "hierarchical structure" versus "common dignity and equality" (See Hubbard, p. 177) but also perhaps to the fact that most members of the Church by reason of gender and/or marital status are excluded from the hierarchical structure and hence do not and cannot participate in any way in the teaching office of the Church and at best marginally in the office of governance? If so, how can this tension be attenuated?

5. Since the ministry of a deacon calls for ordination, should the pastoral care of a parish also call for the sacramental grace of orders? Would it be appropriate to ordain lay parish leaders, when experience had manifested their gifts for such ministry, and their acceptance by the community?

6. What are the possibilities of examining the celebration of the eucharist as a theological locus for the wonderful example of collaboration between ordained and lay ministers?

7. Does the teaching of the New Testament hold that ordinarily a baptized Christian will be involved in some public ministry of the church, at some time?

8. What is the relationship between the call of the baptized to further the mission of the Church in the marketplace and the call to ecclesial lay ministry? Is the former the primary call of the baptized?

9. A clarification of the difference/similarity of the call (vocation) to the ordained ministry and the call (vocation) to the lay ministry. Is lay ministry considered vocation or profession or service or all of these? Does part-time, volunteer lay ministry have the same theological status as full time, paid professional lay ministry?

10. What role should the experience of those who are permanent deacons and those in formation for that order have in a discussion of ministries?

11. What types of ministries can fill the needs of the Catholic community? As the needs are different in nature, so must be the ministries. Name them; describe them.

12. Indicate how such ministries (those that meet the needs of the Catholic community) can be created or encouraged to grow within the existing structures, or suggest new (but feasible) structures.

13. What is the proper understanding of the difference between the baptismal priesthood and the ordained priesthood? Is there a consensus on this understanding?

14. What is the relationship between ELM and ordained ministry? What is specific to each and how do their domains intersect?

15. A key practical issue, viz., a collaborative spirit on the part of the ordained pastors vis-à-vis ELMs, is also a theological one: What needs to be said about a theology of ordained ministry to lead to harmony and healthy ecclesial growth?

16. What is the relationship between ordination and leadership? Is the charism of leadership in the church marked by ordination? What are the implications of this discussion for ecclesial lay ministry? Does the question of access to ordination influence the emergence of lay ministries?

17. What are the needs of the Catholic community that ELM can fill? The correct starting point must be the existing needs of the community.

18. How do we assess the development of ecclesial ministry on this continent in light of cultural realities of our heritage and present age?

19. Several of the papers mention *diversity* and argue that diversity is a gift of and to the Church. It would be helpful to have an explicit definition of what *diversity* is. What do we mean by diversity? Are we open to the gifts and challenges that diversity presents to us?

20. Since ecclesial lay ministers frequently feel undervalued, would it be wise or not to articulate the distinction between those who work for the church in contrast to all the baptized? Since ministry flows from baptism, what is the nature of or what are the underpinnings of shared responsibility/coresponsibility in pastoral activity between the ordained and lay ministers? What ecclesiology needs to be operative for shared responsibility to be effective?

21. Is it possible to determine with greater theological precision the difference between the *ministerial priesthood* and the *priesthood of the faithful*? For more than thirty years, we have lived with the statement that these two "differ essentially and not only in degree." Are we able to offer more precisely what exactly this difference is—beyond what we can already say?

22. The traditional binomial "priest-laity" does not reflect adequately the nature of ministry in the Church, yet it is deeply ingrained in the thinking of Catholics at every level. How can the Church replace a dichotomy that has become sterile with a more theologically sound concept of ministry—one that balances charism and order (hierarchy) in a manner that responds to today's and tomorrow's need for a Church ministerially equipped and structured to evangelize?

23. The church has great difficulty in accomplishing its mission in the world today because its ministerial structures continue to reflect the "priest-laity" conception. The result is a weak and ineffective ministerial presence in many areas of life and an inability to serve adequately the community of believers (those born into Catholic families), let alone reach out to others.

24. How are ecclesial lay ministries related to (a) the ecclesial community, that is, parish or diocese; (b) the other ministries of the faithful; (c) the ministry of ordained pastors; and (d) the ministry and authority of the bishop of the diocese?

Group C: Theologizing from the Present Experience, Focusing on the Signs of the Times

1. In light of biblical testimony to the early Church's readiness to permit new forms of ministry (e.g., Stephen) and also its readiness to recognize the Spirit's gifts in non-Jews (e.g., Cornelius) and women (e.g., Phoebe), by what criteria should we analyze and assess today's emergence of lay ministries?

2. The theology and ministry within the Church of ethnic and gender diversity are still evolving. How can a clear theology of ecclesial lay ministry emerge when the whole is still in process?

3. What guidance for reflection do we get from the example of development in churches on other continents?

4. Relation to feminism: Should a theology of ecclesial lay ministry explicitly take into account feminist concerns? For example, how is ELM correlated—negatively or positively—with the vocation to the permanent diaconate? With rejection of hierarchical structure? With perception of lay roles as passive?

5. Given all the papers presented, which do you consider to be the most basic points of agreement concerning ecclesial lay ministry? To what degree can these be used to establish a theological basis for ELM? Which do you consider to be the most basic points of disagreement? In what ways can these be addressed effectively?

Group D: Appropriateness of Forms of Ecclesial Sponsorship and Recognition

1. Are there structures that would encourage, support, and balance "hierarchical" and "ecclesial lay" ministries to their mutual benefit? What are such structures? How can we develop them?

2. Should there be some common basic training expected of all ecclesial lay ministers, regardless of their specific service in the Church?

3. What is the necessary theological formation for any ecclesial minister, and for particular roles?

4. What should be the relationship of members of such (a) group(s) to the bishop?

5. Do ecclesial lay ministers have an inherent right to support? Or is it the specific situation of each person that determines whether or not he or she is entitled to support?

6. Given the Church's mission of witnessing to the coming of God's kingdom (see *Gaudium et Spes*), what is being expressed theologically in the Church's current labor policies and practices for ecclesial lay ministers?

7. The relatively low percentage of African American and Hispanic American ecclesial lay ministers is of concern. Do you think there is anything theologians can do to help increase the number of African Americans and Hispanic Americans involved in lay ministry?

8. Regarding ecclesial lay ministries: How is a call recognized? How is the call validated? By whom is it validated?

9. Do we need to articulate in a new way the "flow chart" that describes the movement of authority and sanctifying power from the Holy Spirit to all those that exercise public power and authority in the Church?

10. Realizing that all ministry belongs to and is under the jurisdiction of the Church, from what authorizing source does ELM flow? from baptism, confirmation, and eucharist? from personal (charismatic) vocation? from official appointment?

11. Governance: How do lay ministers represent the bishop and relate to him?

12. How are lay ministers to be recognized? certification? commissioning? What is the theological rationale for this?

13. Is some liturgical form of recognition of the assumption of these ministries appropriate? If so, why? If not, why not? If so, what form?

Group E: Evolution of Magisterial Teaching on the Laity in and Since Vatican II

1. Does the "secular character" that LG, no. 31, says is "proper and special to lay people" so ontologically define them that their ministry "in the Church" must always be considered exceptional and supplying for the deficiency of ordained ministers? Or is this secular character a more sociological description of the situation of the majority of lay people?

2. Have we emphasized the conciliar teaching adequately as it shows forth the priesthood of the faithful? Are we somewhat reluctant in reclaiming the full understanding of the priesthood of the faithful lest it impinge on the ministry of the ordained?

3. Is church governance and jurisdiction really able to be exercised by the laity, or does it always have to be a sharing in—participation in—a delegation by the ordained minister, who alone can have jurisdiction because of sacred orders?

4. How are we to understand the relationship between Vatican II's teachings for the Church's renewal and the emergence of today's lay ministries?

5. A theology of lay ministry must take full account of the teaching of Vatican II on the charisms of the faithful, especially as found in LG, nos. 12 and 30; AA, no. 3 and PO, no. 9. Among other things, the council says that from the reception of charisms there follow the right and the duty to use them in the Church and in the world (AA, no. 3). How are such "rights and duties" to be understood?

6. When much ELM is being performed by women religious, what does it mean to say that the ministry of lay persons must be exercised "in conformity with their specific lay vocation" (cf. CL, no. 23)? Are we dealing here with the two different meanings of "lay person" that are found in Vatican II as in LG, nos. 31 and 43?

7. Is it accurate to say that the revised *Code of Canon Law* has given to lay persons the power of governance in some specific cases? Is this a return to an understanding prevalent in the apostolic Church?

8. How do we (clergy, religious, and laity) articulate and appropriate the profound teachings elucidated in the New Testament, *Lumen Gentium, Apostolicam Actuositatem, Code of Canon Law, Christifideles Laici,* and *Called and Gifted for the Third Millennium*? What efforts are being made in formation programs for seminarians, clergy, religious, and laity to prepare all ecclesial ministers for the contemporary reality?

9. Is this ministry rooted in baptism, and does it conform to the understanding of the role of the laity in the Church? How does it relate to *Lumen Gentium's* definition of the secular character of lay mission?

    Is there a good reason for distinguishing between the *munus* of lay persons and a *deputatio ad officium*? If so, where does ecclesial lay ministry belong? If not, how do we situate it within the charisms and offices that come with Christian initiation?

Group F: Ecclesial Lay Ministry within the Context of the Church as Communion, Hierarchy, and Spirit-led

1. If the principle "the one who presides over the community presides over its Eucharist" is valid, then is not the concept of a "parish leader" or "parish life coordinator" (*in effect* a pastor) who cannot preside over the community's eucharist an oxymoron? Furthermore, if the number of priestless parishes with "parish leaders" continues to grow significantly, how will the Church be able to prevent the ministry of the priest from being more and more restricted to the celebration of sacraments?

2. What can theologians do to make the relationship between ecclesiology of *communio* and ecclesiastical hierarchy clearer?

3. Is the expansion of ministries in North American parishes and dioceses in the past twenty-five years a temporary situation that will pass away shortly?

4. Does the New Testament model suggest greater spontaneity than is possible in the contemporary Church?

5. In the light of Bergant's biblical survey, is it correct to describe leadership "from below" as "congregationalist"?—or are we in fact witnessing a new paradigm that mirrors the ecclesiology of First Corinthians?

6. What is the appropriate theological distinction between the ministries arising from baptism and those derived from a hierarchic mandate?

7. How does one articulate the interrelatedness of the common priesthood of all the faithful rooted in baptism and the ministerial priesthood rooted in ordination (LG, no. 10) without blurring the essential distinction between the two on the one hand and without so separating them that a new clericalism emerges on the other?

8. Describe the reciprocal interrelatedness of the common and ministerial priesthood in terms of an ecclesiology of *communio* that situates ordained ministry squarely within the community of believers. Explore in greater depth how *communio* allows for the simultaneous expression of sacramental equality and hierarchical order.

9. Charismatic foundations: In what way is ecclesial lay ministry a vocation? To what extent does it give expression to the aspirations to service and ecclesial functions associated traditionally with vowed religious? How does it differ? What are the implications for religious and lay ministers?

10. What sort of ecclesiological elaboration of ecclesial lay ministry will help to overcome the incipient trend toward "congregationalism" without being perceived as authoritarian?

11. Is jurisdiction and governance a major issue or is equality of persons and leaders (ordained/nonordained) better established by the manner in which collaboration of ministers is developed and worked out?

12. Given the axiom that grace supposes and perfects nature, what is the relationship between charism and competence? Does charism presuppose and work through competence? Does competence make one a candidate for a particular charism or ministry? Does the Spirit give charisms to those without competence and withhold charisms from those with competence?

13. How can an enhanced pneumatology strengthen our understanding of ELM, indeed of all forms of ministry?

14. How should the evolution of these ministries be linked with the growth of ecclesial community as a participatory organism?

15. Ecclesiological/sacramental foundations: How can a theology of ecclesial lay ministry be grounded in an ecclesiology of communion? For example: How do all the baptized/confirmed exercise responsibility for the Church's mission? How do married couples exercise responsibility for the Church's mission? How do the ordained—bishops, priests, and deacons—exercise responsibility for the Church's mission? What functions are "proper" to each?

16. If we accept the implications of the ecclesiology of communion as essential to understanding the post-Vatican II development of lay ministry, how does this affect the possibility for true mutuality, complementarity, and effective collaboration between laity and clergy, and how will we address governance issues?

17. Can we trace in more understandable terms the role and the importance of *koinonia* in the development and the implementation of ecclesial lay ministries in the Church?

Colloquium Participants

Participants

Reverend John Beal, J.C.D., The Catholic University of America

Dianne Bergant, CSA, Ph.D., Catholic Theological Union

Louise Bond, SNJM, D.Min., National Association of Lay Ministers

Most Reverend Tod D. Brown, STB, M.A., Bishop of Boise, Idaho, Former Chair, NCCB Committee on the Laity

Donald W. Buggert, O. Carm., S.T.D., Washington Theological Union

Sara Butler, MSBT, S.T.L., Ph.D., Mundelein Seminary

Allan Figueroa Deck, SJ, S.T.D., Ph.D., Loyola Marymount University

Most Reverend Joseph Delaney, S.T.L., M.A., D.D., Bishop of Fort Worth, Texas

Zoila Diaz, D.Min., St. John Vianney College Seminary

Most Reverend John Dunne, M.A., D.D., Auxiliary Bishop of Rockville Centre, N.Y., Chair, NCCB Committee on Women in Society and in the Church

Sharon Euart, RSM, J.C.D., Associate General Secretary, National Conference of Catholic Bishops

Zeni Fox, Ph.D., Immaculate Conception Seminary

Francis Cardinal George, OMI, Ph.D., Archbishop of Chicago, Ill.

Most Reverend F. Joseph Gossman, J.C.D., Bishop of Raleigh, N.C.

Most Reverend Bernard J. Harrington, M.Div., D.D., Auxiliary Bishop of Detroit, Mich., Member, NCCB Subcommittee on Lay Ministry

James Heft, SM, Ph.D., University of Dayton

Monika Hellwig, Ph.D., Association of Catholic Colleges and Universities

Juan Lorenzo Hinojosa, Ph.D., Hillenbrand Institute, Center for Development in Ministry

Most Reverend James Hoffman, D.D., J.C.L., Bishop of Toledo, Ohio, Member, NCCB Subcommittee on Lay Ministry

Most Reverend Howard Hubbard, D.D., Bishop of Albany, N.Y.

Most Reverend Gerald Kicanas, S.T.L., Ph.D., Auxiliary Bishop of
Chicago, Ill., Member, NCCB Subcommittee on Lay Ministry
Most Reverend Edward Kmiec, S.T.L., D.D., Bishop of Nashville,
Tenn., Member, NCCB Subcommittee on Lay Ministry
Most Reverend William J. Levada, S.T.D., Archbishop of
San Francisco, Calif.
William McConville, OFM, Ph.D., Siena College
Cecilia Moore, Ph.D., University of Dayton
Thomas O'Meara, OP, Ph.D., University of Notre Dame
Ladislas Orsy, SJ, D.C.L., Georgetown University
Paul Philibert, OP, S.T.D., University of Notre Dame
Most Reverend Daniel Pilarczyk, S.T.D., Ph.D., Archbishop of
Cincinnati, Ohio
David Power, OMI, S.T.D., The Catholic University of America
Elissa Rinere, CP, J.C.D., Archdiocese of Los Angeles, Calif.
Most Reverend Phillip F. Straling, M.S., D.D., Bishop of Reno,
Nev., Chair, NCCB Subcommittee on Lay Ministry
Francis A. Sullivan, SJ, S.T.D., Boston College
Most Reverend Emil Wcela, S.T.L., M.A., D.D., Auxiliary Bishop of
Rockville Centre, N.Y., Member, NCCB Subcommittee on Lay
Ministry
Most Reverend G. Patrick Ziemann, M.Div., D.D., Bishop of Santa
Rosa, Calif., Chair, NCCB Committee on the Laity
Jean Marie Hiesberger, Facilitator
Loughlan Sofield, ST, Facilitator
Kathleen Cahalan, Ph.D., Lilly Endowment

Staff
National Conference of Catholic Bishops
    Secretariat for Family, Laity, Women and Youth
    Bishops' Committee on the Laity
    Bishops' Subcommittee on Lay Ministry
        H. Richard McCord, Executive Director
        Ana Villamil, Associate Director
        Sheila Garcia, Assistant Director
        Amy Hoey, RSM, Project Coordinator, Ecclesial Lay Ministry
    Secretariat for Doctrine and Pastoral Practices
    Bishops' Committee on Doctrine
        Siobhan Verbeek, Associate Director
    Secretariat for the Permanent Diaconate
    Bishops' Committee for the Diaconate
        Deacon John Pistone, Executive Director